Monitoring Progress towards a Resource-Efficient and Circular Economy

OECD
BETTER POLICIES FOR BETTER LIVES

Please cite this publication as:
OECD (2024), *Monitoring Progress towards a Resource-Efficient and Circular Economy*, OECD Publishing, Paris, https://doi.org/10.1787/3b644b83-en.

ISBN 978-92-64-32481-7 (print)
ISBN 978-92-64-63688-0 (PDF)
ISBN 978-92-64-45559-7 (HTML)
ISBN 978-92-64-66172-1 (epub)

Photo credits: Cover adapted from © ArtHead, anna.spoka/Shutterstock.com.

Corrigenda to OECD publications may be found on line at: www.oecd.org/about/publishing/corrigenda.htm.

Foreword

Policies that foster the transition towards a more resource efficient and circular economy are gaining significant traction. They are essential for a sustainable, low carbon development and for a competitive economy. These developments bring about demands for reliable information to track progress and gauge results and for indicators that speak to policy makers and the public at large.

The OECD has been supporting its member and partner countries in implementing effective policies for waste and materials management, improving their performance and providing reliable information to the public, decision-makers and authorities. Major tools for implementing shared policy objectives and advancing good practices in these areas are OECD legal instruments. The *Recommendation on Resource Productivity* calls for improving resource productivity and reducing negative environmental impacts of materials and product use. It recommends that Adherents promote integrated life-cycle-oriented approaches, develop and promote the use of indicators for assessing the efficiency of material resource use, and improve and use internationally compatible material flow accounts. The *Recommendation on Environmental Information and Reporting* calls for a comprehensive approach to environmental information and reporting. It recommends that Adherents improve the quality and policy relevance of data, statistics, and derived indicators on the environment and sustainable development, and develop and use sets of policy-relevant and reliable indicators to measure environmental performance and progress towards sustainable development, and to integrate environmental and economic decision-making.

This report presents a conceptual framework and indicators to monitor progress and inform circular economy policies and initiates a reflection on novel data sources and measurement methods that could help fill information gaps. It is designed to support OECD work on circular economy and provides a source of inspiration for countries seeking to build a coherent circular economy monitoring framework.

The report was prepared under the work programme of the OECD Environment Policy Committee (EPOC) and its Working Parties on Resource Productivity and Waste (WPRPW) and on Environmental Information (WPEI). The conceptual monitoring framework and the proposed list of indicators were developed with the OECD Resource Efficiency and Circular Economy Expert Group (RECE-XG) in co-operation with the UNECE Task Force on Measuring Circular Economy (UNECE-TF).

The authors of the report are Myriam Linster, Frithjof Laubinger and Peter Börkey. Shardul Agrawala, Head of the Environment and Economy Integration Division, and Nathalie Girouard, Head of the Environmental Performance and Information Division of the OECD Environment Directorate, provided oversight and guidance.

The work benefitted from the contributions and comments of members of the RECE-XG, members of the UNECE-TF, and delegates of the WPRPW and the WPEI. The financial support of The Netherlands, Finland and the United States of America is gratefully acknowledged.

Table of contents

FIGURES

TABLES

BOXES

Reader's guide

This report was prepared by the OECD Secretariat with the support of the informal OECD Expert Group on a new generation of information for a resource efficient and circular economy (RECE-XG) established by the Working Parties on Environmental Information (WPEI) and on Resource Productivity and Waste (WPRW) and in close co-operation with the UNECE Task Force on measuring circular economy (UNECE-TF). It draws on and leverages OECD experience in the development and use of indicators in policy analysis and evaluation and takes into account relevant activities of countries and other international organisations and their expert groups (including EEA, Eurostat, ISO, UNCEEA, UNEP) as available in October 2023.

The *OECD Expert Group on a new generation of information for a resource efficient and circular economy* (RECE-XG) was set-up as a joint effort of the WPEI and the WPRPW, following on work in 2019-20 on a new generation of information on waste and materials management. It convened on an ad hoc basis between 2021 and 2023, with the purpose to assist the OECD Secretariat in developing better information and practical guidance to support policies for a transition to a resource efficient and circular economy, whilst exploiting synergies with national and international efforts.

The work of the RECE-XG was closely coordinated with the work of the *UNECE Task Force on Measuring the Circular Economy* (UNECE-TF) that proceeded in parallel. The OECD has been leading the work on the policy background, the conceptual monitoring framework and related indicators with inputs by the UNECE-TF. The UNECE has been leading the work on the statistical framework, definitions and classifications, and the links to the SEEA with inputs from the OECD.

Members of the RECE-XG included delegates from the WPEI and the WPRPW, as well as representatives from international organisations and NGOs. Members of the UNECE-TF include country experts and representatives from international organisations (EEA, Eurostat, FAO, IMF, UNECE, UNEP, UNITAR, UNSD, OECD) and NGOs (PACE, WRI).

The content of this report, including a definition for a circular economy, the conceptual monitoring framework, the criteria for selecting indicators and validating their choice, and the proposed list of indicators have been elaborated by consensus during individual and joint meetings of these groups.

Purpose and audience

This report presents a harmonised conceptual framework and indicators for monitoring progress and supporting the implementation of policies that foster a transition towards a more resource efficient and circular economy. Its *main purpose* is to provide a source of inspiration for countries seeking to build a coherent framework to assess progress towards a circular economy and to support OECD and, where appropriate, other international work on a circular economy.

The *main audiences* are ministries, government agencies and statistical offices involved in the preparation and evaluation of policies that encourage a resource-efficient and circular economy, in the measurement of progress towards a CE and in the development and communication of related indicators.

This report is not a statistical compilation guide and does not create any requirements for implementation in countries. It rather provides general guidance for a harmonised monitoring through indicators and advocates the development of a coordinated measurement and indicator research agenda and a phased measurement approach to allow for countries with different capacities to engage in the production of CE data and indicators.

The monitoring framework and indicators presented in this report are *a first step towards better information on the transition to a resource efficient and circular economy*. The list of indicators will be regularly reviewed and refined as better data become available and the implementation and monitoring of circular economy policies in countries progress. The framework and its indicator set are supported with a statistical framework, consistent with the System of Environmental-Economic Accounting (SEEA) where possible, to help structure and combine underlying statistics, to link CE terms and definitions to the terms and definitions used in official statistics, and to ensure coherence among data sets (UNECE, 2024[1]).

Content and structure

The report is structured as follows[1]:

- Chapter 1 introduces the need for a comprehensive and coherent circular economy monitoring framework, in the context of the evolving policy landscape.
- Chapter 2 describes the scope and mechanisms of a circular economy and provides a definition for use in international work.
- Chapter 3 describes the scope and structure of the conceptual monitoring framework.
- Chapter 4 lists the indicator set for use in OECD work, along a 3-tier structure of core, complementary and contextual indicators.
- Chapter 5 dwells upon major measurement gaps for the different dimensions of the framework and initiates a reflection on novel data sources and innovative measurement approaches that could be drawn upon to fill these gaps.
- Chapter 6 concludes with priority areas suggested for further work and practical guidance that could become part of a coordinated measurement and indicator research agenda.
- Annex A presents a detailed list of the proposed indicator set.
- Annex B presents examples of national and international frameworks for monitoring progress towards a resource efficiency and a circular economy.
- Annex C gives an overview of the key principles of OECD work on indicators.

Note

[1] Chapters 1 to 4 served as a basis for the joint UNECE/OECD guidelines on measuring circular economy whose first part (Part A). It was endorsed by the Conference of European Statisticians (CES) in June 2023 subject to comments received and published on 23 February 2024. More detailed practical guidance on the statistical measurement of a circular economy is being prepared with the support of the UNECE-TF.

Aggregates and abbreviations

Abbreviation	Name
3R	Reduce, reuse, recycle
CBS	Statistics Netherlands
CE	Circular Economy
CEPA	Classification of Environmental Protection Activities and Expenditure
CML	Circularity Metrics Lab
COFOG	Classification of the Functions of Government
CReMA	Classification of Resource Management Activities
DANE	Colombian Administrative Department of Statistics
DMC	Domestic Material Consumption
DMI	Domestic Material Input
DRS	Deposit-refund system
EEA	European Environment Agency
EGSS	Environmental Goods and Services Sector Accounts
EMF	Ellen MacArthur Foundation
EoL	End-of-life
EPR	Extended Producer Responsibility
EU-MF	EU Monitoring Framework
FAO	UN Food and Agriculture Organization
FDI	Foreign Direct Investment
GHG	greenhouse gas
HDI	Human Development Index
IFCMA	Inclusive Forum on Carbon Mitigation Approaches
ISIC/NACE	ISIC is the International Standard Industrial Classification of all economic activities. NACE is the acronym used to designate the statistical classification of economic activities in the European Union. The term NACE is derived from the French title: **N**omenclature statistique des **a**ctivités économiques dans la **C**ommunauté **e**uropéenne.

Abbreviation	Name
ISO	International Organization for Standardization
LCA	Life-cycle assessments
MOEJ	Ministry of Environment Japan
ODA	Official Development Assistance
OECD CEI	OECD Core Set of Environmental Indicators
OECD GGI	OECD Green Growth Indicators
OECD MFRP	OECD Material Flow and Resource Productivity Indicators
OECD RECE-XG	OECD Resource Efficiency and Circular Economy Expert Group
PAYT	Pay-as-you-throw
PSUT	physical supply and use tables
PSR	pressure-state-response
R&D	Research and Development
RMC	Raw Material Consumption
RMe	Raw Material equivalents
SDG	Sustainable Development Goals
SEEA	System of Environmental-Economic Accounting
UNCEEA	United Nations Committee of Experts on Environmental-Economic Accounting
UNDESA	United Nations Department of Economic and Social Affairs
UNECE-TF	United Nations Economic Commission for Europe Task Force on Measuring Circular Economy
UNECE-TF WP3	UNECE Task Force Working Package 3
UNEP	UN Environment Programme
UNEP IRP	UNEP International Resource Panel
UNSD	United Nations Statistics Division
WEEE	Waste from Electrical and Electronic Equipment

Executive summary

Waste management and related policies have been moving towards preventive and integrated approaches, emphasising the life-cycle of materials and products. This is reflected in circular economy (CE) initiatives that have emerged at the international, as well as national and sub-national levels across the world. The rise in CE policy initiatives has brought about stronger demands for reliable and more granular information to track progress towards a more resource-efficient and circular economy with improved social and environmental outcomes. It has also raised questions as to the adequacy of the data and indicators currently available.

This report presents a conceptual framework and a set of indicators for monitoring progress towards a resource-efficient and circular economy. The purpose is to provide a harmonised guide for countries seeking to build up a coherent CE monitoring framework and to support international work on the transition to a CE.

As there is great variety in CE definitions, this report proposes a common language and a headline definition that is general enough to serve both measurement and policy needs. It points to three interrelated features and is accompanied by simple explanatory notes and references to the mechanisms and strategies underlying a CE.

> *A circular economy is an economy where the value of materials in the economy is maximised and maintained for as long as possible; the input of materials and their consumption is minimised; the generation of waste is prevented and negative environmental impacts reduced throughout the life-cycle of materials.*

The conceptual monitoring provided in this report is designed to organise thinking about indicators, identify relevant metrics and ensure that nothing important gets overlooked. It links the main features of the CE with the basic principles of accounting and the pressure-state-response (PSR) model used in environmental reporting and assessment. The framework is further designed to be applied at different levels and geographical areas (multilevel monitoring).

The framework has four main interlinked components:

- The *material life-cycle and value chain* component reflects key features and major outcomes of a CE, considering the circularity principle and the various CE mechanisms. It describes the various stages of the material life-cycle and the results of strategies in place to keep the value of materials in the commercial cycle for as long as possible.
- The *interactions with the environment* component describes major environmental and natural resource implications considering the full lifecycle of materials. It links to the ultimate goal of a CE: the preservation of natural capital (natural resources, environmental quality) and human health.
- The *responses and actions* component describes policy responses (environmental, economic, sectoral, social) and other societal responses and actions that could drive the transition to a CE and create opportunities for socio-economic development.

- Finally, the *socio-economic opportunities* component describes the social and economic outcomes of the transition to a CE, taking into account aspects of economic efficiency and social equity that are central to a just transition.

The indicator set provided in this report is defined in a 3-tier structure that assesses each indicator against its relevance, analytical soundness and measurability and categorises them as "core-", "complementary-" and "contextual indicators". The proposed *core indicators* aim to capture key elements of a CE, respond to main CE policy questions and point to developments or changes that may require further analysis and possible action. *Complementary indicators* accompany the message conveyed by "core" indicators, provide additional detail, or cover additional aspects. *Contextual indicators* provide background information on socio-economic and environmental variables and facilitate interpretation in the appropriate country context. Whilst countries may consider adapting the set of indicators to their own needs, the size of the set should remain manageable with no more than 20-25 core indicators.

Measurement issues and data gaps exist for several indicators included in the set. As measuring progress towards a CE has become a dynamic field with many national and international initiatives, good international co-ordination is essential. What is needed is a *co-ordinated indicator research agenda* and a pragmatic, step-wise approach to improving measurement in countries accompanied with statistical guidance and a regular exchange of good practices.

Among the areas to be given priority are improvements in waste statistics and material flow accounts, the production of better data on the various CE business models and their effects, better use of accounting frameworks and the generation of data on upstream actions (e.g. waste prevention, reuse and repair activities).

Other opportunities that countries and international organisations can explore to fill some of the data gaps include (1) strengthening the use and usefulness of official statistics and data sources from international organisations and national administrations; (2) exploiting alternative and novel data sources that go beyond official statistics, such as data from the private sector and trade associations; and (3) making use of innovative data sourcing techniques and data collection tools (e.g. Internet of Things (IoT) devices, web-scraping, digital fingerprints or search engine trends). Insights from these developments will help further refine and specify the indicator set and facilitate its use in policy development and evaluation.

1 Introduction

Waste management and related policies have in the past decades been moving towards preventive and integrated approaches, with emphasis on the life-cycle of materials and products. This is reflected in 3R "reduce, reuse, recycle" policies, resource productivity and sustainable materials management programmes, and in circular economy initiatives that gained significant political traction in recent years. Increasing attention is given to specific materials, waste streams and components that raise concerns as to the environmental and health impacts of their management and use or the security of their supply. Examples include food, plastics, electric and electronic products, or construction and demolition waste, hazardous materials, or critical metals.

These developments brought about stronger demands for reliable and more granular information to track progress towards a more resource efficient and circular economy. This includes *inter alia* information on waste generation and management, the value and supply chains of materials and products, the circularity of material flows in the economy, the underlying drivers and related socio-economic outputs and environmental implications. It also raised questions as to the adequacy of the data and indicators currently available for effectively supporting national policies and international work.

This report is *a first step towards better information on a resource efficient and circular economy*. It presents a harmonised conceptual framework and indicators for monitoring progress and supporting the development and evaluation of policies that foster a transition towards a circular economy (CE). The purpose is to assist countries seeking to build a coherent framework to assess progress towards a CE, and to support OECD and other international work on a CE. This report is not a statistical compilation guide. It rather provides general guidance for a harmonised monitoring through indicators and advocates the development of an *indicator research agenda* to improve information on a CE in a coordinated way and a *phased implementation* to allow for countries with different capacities to engage in the production of CE data and indicators.

The monitoring framework and indicators presented in this report will be regularly reviewed and refined as better data become available and the implementation and monitoring of circular economy policies in countries progress. They are supported with a statistical framework, consistent with the System of Environmental-Economic Accounting (SEEA) where possible, to help structure and combine underlying statistics, to link CE terms and definitions to the terms and definitions used in official statistics, and to ensure coherence among data sets (see (UNECE, 2024[1])). More detailed statistical and methodological guidance is being prepared with the support of the UNECE Task Force on Measuring Circular Economy.

2 Defining a circular economy to guide the monitoring of progress

A variety of policy frameworks, targets and specific policy instruments have been developed and implemented at sub-national, national and multilateral levels. Several countries have developed strategies, roadmaps and policy packages that address resource efficiency using a circular economy approach. Resource efficiency and circular economy objectives may also be included in national reform programmes or in national innovation strategies.

Several high-profile multilateral initiatives have emerged. The G7 Alliance on Resource Efficiency was established at Schloss Elmau in 2015 and has been built upon by the adoption of the Toyama Framework on Material Cycles in 2016, and the Bologna Roadmap in 2017. In 2017, G20 governments established the ongoing G20 Resource Efficiency Dialogue. The Circular Economy Action Plan released in 2020 forms one of the main building blocks of the 2020 European Green Deal. Resource productivity and the circular economy are one of the top priorities for the work of the OECD on environmental policies (OECD, 2019[2]; OECD, 2022[3]). Similarly, the OECD Recommendation of the Council on Resource Productivity aims to encourage sustainable resource management and limit environmental impacts associated with the use of resources (OECD, 2008[4]).

The type and scope of the information needed to support CE policies depend on *how a CE is defined* and on the *purpose* for which the information is needed, such as policy development, policy monitoring and evaluation, awareness raising, communication, participation. They also depend on whether the information is to be used in international work or to support national or regional policies and initiatives.

CE policies can address a breadth of topics and mechanisms. It is therefore important to clarify the scope of the monitoring and its statistical boundaries, and to build a consensus on a common language and a definition that can guide the monitoring of progress at international level and the development of a harmonised indicators framework that interested countries can adapt to their own circumstances.

2.1. Scope and objectives of policies for a circular economy

Countries can have different rationales to increasing resource efficiency and establishing a circular economy. Hence the scope of CE objectives and policies varies across countries.

CE policies typically cut across environmental issues and policy domains. They are often seen as a means to address other environmental issues (e.g. climate change), improve supply security of energy and materials, and increase resource efficiency in production and consumption. Whilst environmental objectives are most prevalent, social and economic objectives are also considered key components of a CE. A transition to a CE is increasingly seen as an opportunity to make an economy more sustainable, competitive and resilient.

CE policies can cover different types of materials and products and many different aspects of the life cycle of materials and their value chains, ranging from material extraction and product design to production and consumption processes, innovation and trade. Waste and materials management, material recovery and raw material consumption are usually core elements, together with energy efficiency for some countries.

Water management and water use efficiency are also sometimes considered, in particular in countries where freshwater resources are scarce. Other aspects often considered include eco-design, green public procurement (GPP), innovation, repair and reuse. Hence, the interlinkages, level of alignment and trade-offs between CE policies and other policies addressing these issues need to be well understood.

The monitoring of progress and the statistical measurement need to take into account the economic, environmental and social dimensions of a CE and its levels of application, including the macro, meso and micro levels, as well as the way materials flow through the economy, and between the economy and the environment. It is furthermore important that the data and statistics produced for different dimensions and levels complement each other and are coherent with each other.

2.2. The concept of a circular economy

The concept of a CE is multi-dimensional. It relates to other concepts and principles, including but not limited to, the so-called R-framework that distinguishes different strategies listed from the "most circular" to the "least circular" (see Box 2.1), the concept of resource productivity or resource efficiency[1] and sustainable materials management. It focuses on the circularity of the material flows[2] and on the socio-economic and environmental benefits that arise from it, the ultimate goal being to lower natural resource extraction and decrease environmental and social impacts without an associated reduction of economic output. A CE is understood to be restorative and regenerative by design and to gradually achieve a decoupling of economic growth from the consumption of finite resources, while meeting human and societal needs.

Box 2.1. The R Framework and the circularity ladder

The number of 'R's featured in the R Framework has evolved over time, from the Japanese Government's '3R Initiative' (reduce, reuse, recycle) in 2004, to the European Union's waste hierarchy in its 2008 Waste Framework Directive featuring four Rs (reduce, reuse, recycle, recover), to ten Rs which constitute the 2017 "Circularity Ladder" (Potting et al., 2017, p. 5[5]):

- *Smarter product use and manufacture* (R0-R2):
    - R0 Refuse: Make product redundant by abandoning its function or by offering the same function with a radically different product.
    - R1 Rethink: Make product use more intensive (e.g., through sharing products, or by putting multi-functional products on the market).
    - R2 Reduce: Increase efficiency in product manufacture or use by consuming fewer natural resources and materials.
- *Extended lifespan of products and their parts* (R3-R7):
    - R3 Reuse: Reuse by another consumer of discarded product which is still in good condition and fulfils its original function.
    - R4 Repair: Repair and maintenance of defective product so it can be used with its original function.
    - R5 Refurbish: Restore an old product and bring it up to date.
    - R6 Remanufacture: Use parts of discarded product in a new product with the same function.
    - R7 Repurpose: Use discarded product or parts of it in a new product with a different function.
- *Useful application of materials* (R08-R09):
    - R8 Recycle: Process materials to the same (high-grade) or lower (low grade) quality.
    - R9 Recover: Incineration of materials with energy recovery.

Figure 2.1. A Circularity Ladder

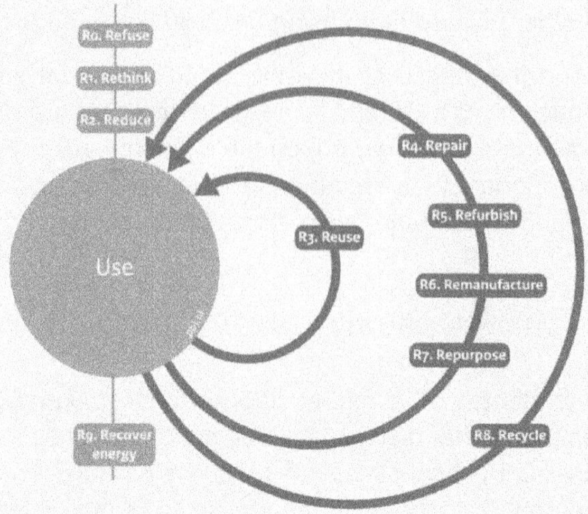

Source: (PBL, 2018[6])

The transition towards a CE is not limited to certain materials or sectors. It is a *systemic change* that affects the entire economy, involves all products and services and is associated with the development and uptake of new business models.

A circular economy operates at different inter-related levels:

- The *micro* level: consumers, products, firms.
- The *meso* level: economic activity sectors, industries, cities, sub-national governments. This level also includes eco-industrial parks, networks and clusters.
- The *macro* level: national economies, countries, as well as supranational entities such as the European Union.

Progressing towards a CE requires the involvement of many stakeholders:

- Governments, who formulate policy objectives and framework conditions that promote changes in the economy and in the society and that ensure policy coherence for a more resource efficient and circular economy.
- Businesses who produce goods and services and are the final responsible entity of making decisions about production conditions and private investments within given framework conditions.
- Consumers who purchase the goods and services produced and whose demand and behaviour are important drivers of a circular economy.
- Other stakeholders such as NGOs that act as advocates of a circular economy and whose actions help raise awareness and facilitate the sharing of information.

There is *no single definition nor terminology* for characterising a CE. Its meaning varies across countries and literature. It depends on the objectives pursued and on the policies put in place. Most definitions in use *have in common the principle of circularity* and the goal of moving away from the traditional linear business models to more circular ones. A core view of a CE is that it can be defined relative to a traditional linear economic system, i.e. one that focuses on "closing" resource loops of current linear resource value chains. A second, slightly broader, view of a CE stresses the importance of "slower material flows", either within an economy with some degree of material circularity, or within an economy that is more linear through product life extension. The third, and broadest, view of a CE is one that involves a more efficient and sustainable use of natural resources, materials, and products within an existing linear system, also including waste prevention (see Explanatory notes on page 17).

2.3. Mechanisms for a circular economy

CE mechanisms may take place at different levels, including different government levels, different firm/sector levels and different geographical areas. They may also cover different time horizons depending on countries' policy objectives.

The OECD distinguishes several mechanisms that contribute at varying degrees to a CE (Figure 2.2). These mechanisms can be related to the R framework (Potting et al., 2017[5]) and to the CE model and circularity strategies used in the Bellagio principles.[3]

- *Closing resource loops* seeks to prevent waste from being generated by substituting virgin materials and new products with secondary raw materials (i.e. from recycled industrial or household waste) and second-hand, repaired or remanufactured products.
- *Slowing resource loops* seeks to slow down consumption and demand for primary raw (virgin) materials by extending the life of existing goods usually thanks to more durable product design. This can be achieved by building long-lasting products that are easy to repair and the ownership of which can change during their lifecycle.
- *Narrowing resource loops and flows* seeks to increase resource efficiency, either by decreasing the total amount of resources used per unit of output or by making better economic use of existing capacity, and achieve a more efficient use of natural resources, materials, and products, either through the development and diffusion of new production technologies, the increased utilisation of existing assets, or shifts in consumption behaviour away from material intensive goods and services. Narrowing a resource flow does not necessarily imply circularity in the form of loops. It can also be implemented within a linear business model by producing products with less materials and thus achieving a higher or equal output with less material input.

CE strategies may also encompass a transition to a bio-based economy with mechanisms that seek to substitute non-renewable materials with sustainably produced renewable materials (European Commission, 2018[7]).

A *transition to a CE* could be seen as involving any process that leads to lower rates of natural resource extraction and use, and to lower negative environmental and social impacts. To the extent that it goes without an associated reduction of economic output, a CE transition can thus result in improved resource efficiency and decoupling.

Figure 2.2. Mechanisms and features of a circular economy

Source: Adapted from (McCarthy, Dellink and Bibas, 2018[8])

2.4. A headline definition

Due to the great variety in CE definitions, it is important to agree on a common language and define a circular economy in a way that guides the development of a harmonised indicator framework. Such a definition should point at the key elements of a CE but be general enough to serve both measurement and policy needs.

This is best achieved by a *hierarchy of definitions* that help converge around common key features, whilst giving sufficient flexibility to further adapt to different needs and circumstances, and to different levels of application (e.g. global, regional, national, sub-national, sectors, industries or firms, products). This hierarchy comprises a *headline definition*[4], which is accompanied by simple *explanatory notes* and references to the mechanisms and strategies underlying a CE, as well as details to guide statistical measurement.

The headline definition highlights *three interrelated features* of a CE, starting with a distinctive feature that refers to maintaining the value of materials in the economy for as long as possible, thus linking to the circularity principle, whilst ensuring a positive outcome to society. The two other features dwell upon particular aspects that link to the concepts of resource productivity and resource efficiency and to the ultimate objective of a CE and whose monitoring is essential: the preservation of natural capital (natural resources, environmental quality) and human health.

The definition is designed for use in international work and can also serve as a reference for interested countries. Its explanatory notes may be revised and supplemented as the CE mechanisms and strategies in countries take shape and develop.

Headline definition

A circular economy is an economy where:

- the value of materials in the economy is maximised and maintained for as long as possible
- the input of materials and their consumption is minimised
- the generation of waste is prevented and negative environmental impacts reduced throughout the life-cycle of materials.

Explanatory notes

- "*Materials*" are understood to include natural resources and the materials and products derived therefrom, i.e. materials at all points throughout their life-cycles (based on OECD/LEGAL/0358).[1] The "*value of materials in the economy*" is understood to encompass the value for society as a whole, taking into account economic efficiency, environmental effectiveness and social equity.
- "*Maintaining the value for as long as possible*" links to the circularity concept and to the higher level R strategies that help close and slow material loops in the economy, such as reuse, repair or remanufacturing.
- "*Minimising the input of materials and their consumption*" links to the concepts of resource productivity and resource efficiency. It is understood to contain both:
    - a *quantitative dimension*, e.g. reducing the quantity of materials extracted from natural resources (virgin materials/primary raw materials, unused extraction) and the quantity of materials used whether from domestic origin or from imports;
    - a *qualitative dimension*, e.g. reducing the use of materials that are potentially damaging to the environment or whose production and consumption processes have negative environmental impacts, and improving the productivity of materials use at all stages of their life-cycle.
    - It links to the preservation, restoration and regeneration of natural assets. Improved resource productivity will also reduce demand pressure on natural resources more generally, and thereby contribute to more secure supplies of natural resources for everyone (OECD/LEGAL/0358).
- The "*life-cycle of materials*" is understood to include all phases of the material cycle such as extraction, transportation, product design, manufacture, final consumption/use, reuse, end-of-life, recovery and final disposal, as well as the associated waste management activities and R strategies.
  By referring to the life-cycle of materials,
    i. Waste prevention at all stages of the life-cycle is reflected and the importance of higher level Rs is highlighted.
       N.B. Waste minimisation and waste prevention entail a quantitative and a qualitative dimension. They encompass activities that reduce both the quantity and the hazardous character of wastes. The scope of waste minimisation is broader than that of waste prevention in that it includes recycling and (if considered appropriate) incineration with energy recovery.
       Waste minimisation is understood to mean: "preventing and/or reducing the generation of waste at the source; improving the quality of waste generated, such as reducing the hazard, and encouraging re-use, recycling, and recovery." (OECD Definition) (OECD, 2000[9])
       Waste prevention is understood to encompass (a) Strict Avoidance, (b) Reduction at Source and (c) Product Re-use. (OECD Definition) (OECD, 2004[10]). It occurs before products/materials are identified or recognised as waste.
       Strict Avoidance involves the complete prevention of waste generation by virtual elimination of hazardous substances or by reducing material or energy intensity in production, consumption, and distribution.
       Reduction at Source involves minimising use of toxic or harmful substances and/or minimising material or energy consumption.
    ii. All associated environmental impacts are reflected, including impacts on natural assets, on climate, on air, water and soil quality, on biodiversity, on human health, as well as underlying pressures in terms of emissions or discharges of pollutants, greenhouse gases, wastewater, and other residuals from production and consumption processes, including natural resource residuals (e.g. unused extraction).

1. This is in line with the definition of "resources" used in the OECD Council Recommendation on Resource productivity (OECD/LEGAL/0358) and the definition of "material resources" used by the UNEP IRP, i.e. biomass (like crops for food, energy and bio- based materials, as well as wood for energy and industrial uses), fossil fuels (in particular coal, gas and oil for energy), metals (such as iron, aluminium and copper used in construction and electronics manufacturing) and non-metallic minerals (used for construction, notably sand, gravel and limestone) (International Resource Panel, 2019[11]).

Notes

[1] Resource productivity refers to "the effectiveness with which an economy or a production process is using natural resources" In line with the Recommendation by the OECD Council on Resource Productivity (OECD/LEGAL/0358) the term "resource productivity" is understood to contain both a quantitative dimension (e.g. the quantity of output produced with a given input of natural resources) and a qualitative dimension (e.g. the environmental impacts per unit of output produced with a given natural resource input).

[2] In line with the Recommendation by the OECD Council on Resource Productivity (OECD/LEGAL/0358) the term "material" is understood to include natural resources and the materials and products derived therefrom.

[3] Elaborated by the European Environment Agency (EEA) and its "Bellagio process" on monitoring progress in Europe's circular economy (in partnership with the Italian Institute for Environmental Protection and Research - ISPRA). (EEA, 2021[13])

[4] The headline definition and its explanatory notes used in this report, are inspired by existing CE definitions in particular previous definitions used by the OECD (McCarthy, Dellink and Bibas, 2018[8]), the definitions used by the European Commission and the European Environment Agency (EEA), and the suggested definition for measurement initially proposed by the UNECE-TF, as well as input from meetings of the OECD RECE-XG and the UNECE-TF.

3 The conceptual monitoring framework

The main purpose of the conceptual monitoring framework is to organise thinking about indicators, to identify relevant metrics and to ensure that nothing important gets overlooked. It reflects the integrated and cross-cutting nature of a CE while organising the indicators in a way useful to decision-makers and the public. It is supported with a statistical framework, consistent with the System of Environmental-Economic Accounting (SEEA) where possible, to help structure and combine underlying statistics, to link CE terms and definitions to the terms and definitions used in official statistics, and to ensure coherence among data sets (UNECE, 2024[1]).

Analysis around the conceptual monitoring framework is expected to also identify the needs for capacity building in developing countries and emerging economies, to consolidate and strengthen their information base on waste and material flows, R strategies and related environmental impacts.

3.1. Scope

The conceptual framework covers all dimensions of a CE and the whole lifecycle of materials, products and services. The principles applied in drawing it up were:

- A *balanced coverage* of the main dimensions of a circular economy and of their main features, aligned with the CE definition in chapter 2.
- The identification of *key aspects* for which indicators are needed, i.e. those that are of common relevance to resource efficiency and circular economy policies in OECD member and partner countries and beyond.
- A *structure* and indicators that could be applied at different levels and geographical areas (multilevel monitoring).

For practical reasons, the monitoring scope in this report focuses on "materials" in line with material flow analysis and accounting, i.e. mineral resources (metallic and non-metallic industrial minerals), biomass, and energy carriers (e.g. coal, oil, gas). Particular attention is given to materials whose extraction, processing, use and disposal are internationally significant, in both economic and environmental terms. This is in line with the definition of the OECD Council Recommendation on Resource Productivity (OECD/LEGAL/0358) and the definition of "material resources" used by the UNEP International Resource Panel. The physical and the monetary aspects of a CE are both considered.

Water resources and energy (beyond energy carriers) are covered to the extent that they are part of an integrated approach to the entire resource cycle and the associated environmental impacts. It is recognised that sustainable use of freshwater and energy resources is conceptually part of a CE. Bulk water flows and circular use of water resources are not within the scope of this report but can easily be integrated by government agencies or national statistical offices. National and international sets of environmental and sustainable development indicators include water-related indicators that can be used for this purpose complemented with circularity indicators. The same applies to energy use and energy efficiency.

3.2. Structure

The conceptual framework combines the main features of a CE with the basic principles of accounting and the pressure-state-response (PSR) model used in environmental reporting and assessment. It has four components centred around the material life-cycle and the economy's production and consumption functions, and describes the interactions with the environment – the natural asset base and environmental quality –, policy actions and the derived socio-economic opportunities that contribute to a just transition (Figure 3.1).

Given the breadth of the topics that need to be covered within the four components, a further structuring is applied by defining indicator themes and topics (Table 3.2).

Figure 3.1. Conceptual monitoring framework – building blocks

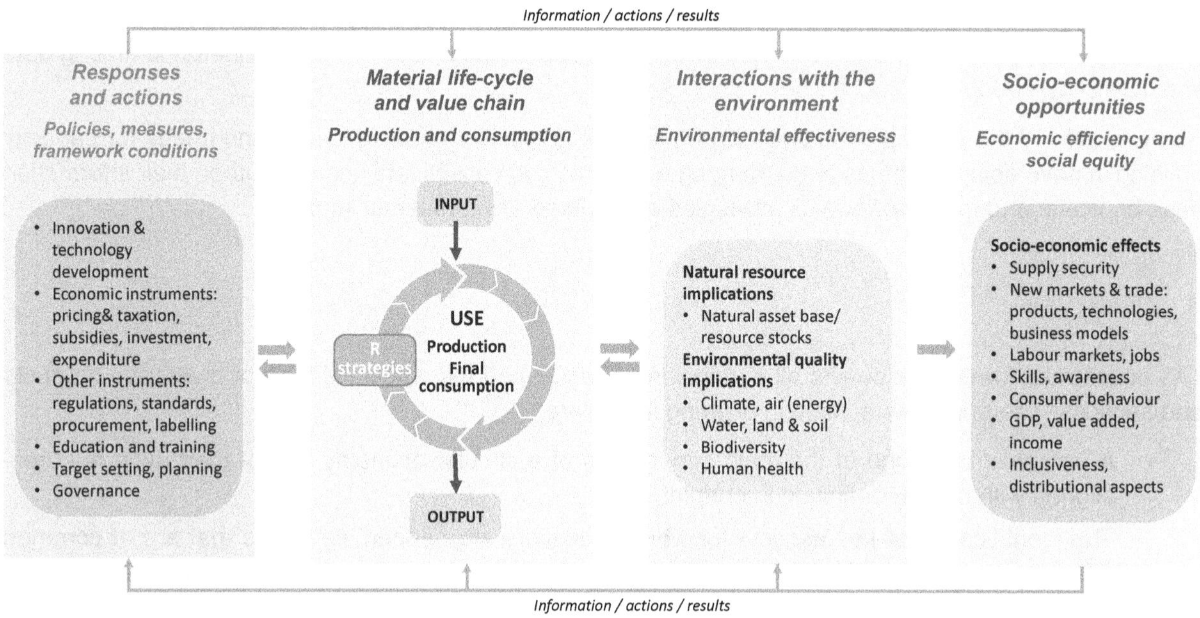

Note: The framework combines the main features of a CE with the basic principles of accounting and the pressure-state-response (PSR) model used in environmental reporting and assessment. It draws on the frameworks used for OECD environmental indicators and green growth indicators, and is inspired by the CE frameworks used in countries (e.g. the Netherlands) and the EU.

3.2.1. Material life-cycle and value chain

This component describes the various stages of the material life-cycle and value chain, from raw material inputs to solid waste outputs, materials use in production and final consumption and the R strategies in place to keep the value of materials in the commercial cycle for as long as possible. It reflects key features and major outcomes of a CE, considering the circularity principle and the various CE mechanisms.

Related indicators show how materials enter, flow within and (eventually) leave the economy. They should lend themselves to being linked to reference values (benchmarks, thresholds, baselines, objectives, targets) and to environmental issues, including climate change, toxic contamination, biodiversity, natural resource management. As a rule, main indicators on the material life cycle should also lend themselves to being related to indicators on responses and actions and to indicators on opportunities to help linking responses to results obtained as a first step in monitoring the effectiveness of policies. They are to be complemented with information and indicators on the factors that drive demand for materials (population growth and structure, household size, economic growth and structure, income levels, final consumption expenditure) and on which policy levers can act.

Given the breadth of the topics to be covered, this building block is further structured around three themes:

- The *material basis and productivity of the economy*, i.e. indicators on the level and characteristics of materials supply and their use in the economy or in industries, paying particular attention to material inputs, including domestic extraction and imports, material consumption, including domestic material consumption and raw material consumption (footprints), and material accumulation in the economy (stocks, addition to stocks), as well as indicators relating materials use to GDP, value-added or other socio-economic output variables through intensity or productivity ratios.
- The *management efficiency of materials and waste, and the circularity of material flows* with reference to R strategies and CE mechanisms when possible. Examples include indicators on waste generation (by source, by type); recycling rates; circular use rates; shares of secondary raw materials in material inputs or consumption; renewable content of material used in production processes, products diverted from the waste stream (repaired, remanufactured, reused); materials leaving the economic cycle, i.e. waste going to final disposal.
- *Interactions with trade and globalisation* (international dimension of a CE), i.e. indicators on exports and imports of materials, second-hand goods, end-of-life products and waste, the physical trade balance and the material intensity of trade.

Indicators under this component could also be grouped in line with the CE mechanisms (closing resource loops, slowing resource loops, narrowing resource flows).

Data availability permitting the selected indicators should be able to:

- distinguish between primary and secondary raw materials;
- distinguish between materials stemming from non-renewable natural assets (or technical materials) and materials stemming from renewable natural assets (or bio-based materials)[1].
- capture developments in materials that raise specific concerns as to:
    - their environmental significance, i.e. their significance with respect to natural resource management and waste and materials management issues, and to the environmental consequences of their production, use or end-of-life management. Examples include pollution from mismanaged products and materials, such as electric and electronic equipment and plastics.
    - their economic importance, i.e. their significance with respect to economic development, supply security, international trade. Examples include strategic raw materials such as certain metals and rare earths, food or energy carriers.

Material-specific indicators provide important information to assess progress in key supply chains.

Relevant indicators can be derived from sets of material flow and resource productivity indicators and from sets of environmental, green growth and sustainable development indicators, complemented with new and improved indicators that capture the circularity of material flows in the economy and in production and consumption processes. Underlying data can be derived from material flow analyses and accounts, waste statistics and accounts, product statistics and trade statistics. The availability of physical supply and use tables (PSUT) would be an advantage, as well as the availability of material-specific flow accounts.

When monitoring policies that promote the circularity and efficiency of water and energy use, related indicators can easily be added under this component.

3.2.2. Interactions with the environment

This component describes major environmental and natural resource implications, considering the full lifecycle of materials. It links to the ultimate goal of a CE: the preservation of natural capital (natural resources, environmental quality) and human health.

The economic activities that drive materials use have a range of environmental consequences. Some of these consequences can be attributed directly to resource provision (e.g. greenhouse gas (GHG) emissions from extraction and processing of primary materials), while others are indirectly linked to resource use, such as air pollution caused by the combustion of fossil fuels (Box 3.1).[2]

Box 3.1. Environmental implications of materials management and use

Different material resources have different characteristics and the activities associated with their extraction, management and use have different environmental implications and potential impacts. Ore mining can cause air and water pollution, waste generation and pressures on biodiversity and habitats. Refining mined ores into metal is energy and water intensive. Fossil fuel exploitation results in pollution and habitat disruption at the extraction sites and carbon dioxide emissions when used in combustion. Non-energy uses of fossil fuels for example in plastics or chemicals have a different set of environmental implications, including the pollution of environmental systems by persistent plastic waste and toxic contamination by chemicals. Unsustainable production of biomass, i.e. farming, fishing and forestry, can contribute to land cover changes, the loss of ecosystem services, biodiversity loss and soil degradation. Deforestation can lead to increased soil erosion, habitat destruction and loss of biodiversity, whilst depleting carbon sinks and thus contributing to global warming (OECD, 2019[2]).

Table 3.1. Potential environmental impacts by material group[1]

Material Group	Potential environmental impacts
Biomass (for food and feed)	Intensification of land use, land cover change, soil degradation, groundwater contamination, disintegration of nutrient cycles, food chain contamination through pesticides, acidification, loss of biodiversity, habitat loss, water use, eutrophication, GHG emissions
Wood	Intensification of land use, soil erosion, loss of biodiversity, forest degradation, habitat alteration, carbon sink depletion, air and GHG emissions (e.g., fuel wood), desertification, alteration of watersheds
Fossil energy carriers	Air pollution, CO_2 and other GHG emissions, habitat alteration, overburden, toxic chemicals for processing, water use
Metals and metal ores	Irreversible ecosystem change (entropy generation), toxicity, habitat alteration, mining overburden, air and GHG emissions, water use, tailings, radioactivity
Industrial minerals	Irreversible ecosystem change (entropy generation), toxicity, habitat alteration, mining overburden, air and GHG emissions, wastewater, tailings
Construction minerals	Loss of biodiversity, habitat alteration, CO_2 emissions (e.g., from cement manufacturing), transport intensity, sealing of land area, soil compaction

1. Potential pressures and impacts from material extraction, processing and use. Does not consider impacts from EoL management.
Source: adapted from (OECD, 2015[12])

This building block is structured into two themes reflecting:

- The *physical evolution of natural assets* recognising that a declining asset base constitutes a risk to growth and well-being. Examples include material extraction rates and changes in natural resource stocks, depletion ratios and regeneration rates (for renewable resources), freshwater abstraction for material extraction, processing and use, as well as natural resource residuals (unused extraction).

- The *environmental and human health impacts* due to materials extraction, processing, use and end-of-life management, including impacts on climate, on air, water and soil quality, on biodiversity, human exposure to these impacts, and the underlying pressures. Examples include material output flows such as greenhouse gas emissions, the carbon footprint of priority materials (e.g. plastics, food), discharges of pollutants and other residuals from production and consumption processes (e.g. air emissions, water discharges) and related effects on human health, impacts from material extraction, processing, use and end-of-life management on land, habitats and species (terrestrial and marine).

Relevant indicators can be derived from sets of environmental, green growth and sustainable development indicators, with some adjustments to be fit for CE purposes. Underlying data can be derived from environmental monitoring systems (e.g. air, water), environment statistics and environmental accounts (e.g. material flow accounts, natural asset accounts, air emission accounts, water accounts, land accounts), complemented with data from earth observation.

When monitoring policies that promote the circularity and efficiency of water and energy use, additional indicators can easily be added under this component.

3.2.3. Responses and actions

This component describes policy responses (environmental, economic, sectoral, social) and other societal responses and actions that could favour a resource-efficient and circular economy, including measures to change awareness and behaviour and to create new socio-economic opportunities (e.g. new markets, education and training, innovation) that help ensure a just transition.

Related indicators cover the variety of policy tools that can encourage a transition towards a CE by setting the right framework conditions, provide incentives towards substituting away from scarce environmental resources and environmentally harmful products, and fostering innovation, productivity and human capital. This includes economic, regulatory and information instruments and partnerships. As a rule, indicators on responses and actions should lend themselves to being related to indicators on the material life cycle and to indicators on opportunities to help linking responses to results obtained as a first step in monitoring the effectiveness of policies.

The measures to be considered are structured as follows:

- Measures to *support or incentivise circular use of materials, promote recycling markets and optimise design*. Examples include:
    - Taxes, subsidies and regulations supporting *circular business models*, (e.g. sharing or product-service-system models); and instruments encouraging reuse, through second-hand markets, repair and remanufacturing.
    - Downstream policy instruments that create incentives for recycling and enhance sorting at source, such as extended producer responsibility (EPR) schemes, deposit-refund and Pay-as-You-Throw (PAYT) schemes.
    - Upstream policy instruments that help restrain demand for primary materials, make recycled materials more price competitive and incentivise design for circularity, extended lifespans, recycling & dismantling, such as recycled content targets, taxes on materials and products that raise particular concerns (e.g. plastics), circular (and green) public procurement, reforms of subsidies encouraging unsustainable use or extraction of materials, bans and guidelines on substances that restrict recycling.
- Measures to *improve the efficiency of waste management and close leakage pathways* such as investments in waste management infrastructure, waste collection and sorting; anti-littering

instruments, including bans or taxes on frequently littered items (e.g. plastics); and instruments that enhance sorting at source, including bans or taxes on landfilling and incineration.

- Measures to *boost innovation and orient technological change* for more (efficient and) circular material lifecycles, enhanced recycling, and reduced leakage of residuals to the environment. Examples include: R&D budgets of governments and businesses; development and international diffusion of CE technologies (e.g. patented inventions related to recycling and secondary raw materials).
- *Target setting and planning,* including resource productivity and recycling targets, targets on recycled content, waste reduction and prevention, landfilling; and the availability of CE plans and strategies.
- Measures to *strengthen domestic and international financial flows* for a CE and reduced leakage of residuals to the environment. Examples include: Business investments in CE activities; government budgets allocated to CE objectives; Official development assistance (ODA) and Foreign Direct Investment (FDI) dedicated to CE activities.
- Measures to *inform, educate and train*, including product and packaging-oriented information instruments and measures such as eco-labelling, certification schemes; integration of CE issues in school curricula and professional training.

Related indicators could also be grouped according to the type of instruments (economic, regulatory, etc.), the targeted objective as described above or in line with the CE mechanisms (closing resource loops, slowing resource loops, narrowing resource flows).

It is recognised that the policy tools and measures listed above do not all lend themselves to being measured by indicators, and that their effectiveness strongly depends on implementation and is context specific. Also, the mere presence of a certain policy only partially informs about progress towards a CE but helps identify trends in policy development and areas where further actions or responses may be needed.

3.2.4. Socio-economic opportunities

This component describes the social and economic outcomes of a transition to a resource efficient and circular economy, taking into account aspects of economic efficiency and social equity that are central to a just transition.

Related indicators capture the development of new markets, trade[3] and employment opportunities, changes in supply security or autonomy[4], levels of education, skills development (closely linked to the capacity to innovate), and behavioural changes (households, consumers, firms). They also capture new developments, which are not visible through broader recycling and material flow indicators, such as the uptake of new circular business models and industrial ecology/symbiosis initiatives with links to entrepreneurship, and sharing economy initiatives, as well as distributional aspects of CE policies and actions, such as environmental justice.

The indicators are structured around four themes:

- Market developments and new business models
- Trade developments
- Skills, awareness and behaviour
- Inclusiveness of the transition

Table 3.2. Overview of framework themes and indicator topics

Framework	Themes	Indicator topics – Aspects to be considered
Material life-cycle and value chain (production and consumption)	**The material basis of the economy** *(level & characteristics of materials supply and their use in the economy)*	• Material inputs and consumption: share of renewable materials, recyclable materials • Material accumulation in the economy
	The circularity of material flows and the management efficiency of materials & waste *(with reference to R strategies and CE mechanisms)*	• Waste generation • Contribution of secondary raw materials to material inputs or consumption • Contribution of renewable or recyclable materials to production processes • Products diverted from the waste stream through repair, remanufacture, reuse • Materials diverted from final disposal through recycling and recovery • Materials leaving the economic cycle
	Interactions with trade	• Material exports, imports, trade balance
Interactions with the environment (environmental effectiveness)	**Natural resource implications** *(physical evolution of natural assets)*	• Material extraction (used) • Natural resource residuals (unused extraction) • Changes in natural resource stocks; extraction rates, depletion ratios • Water abstracted for material extraction and processing • Intensity of use of forest resources
	Environmental quality implications *(effects of materials extraction, processing, use and end of life management on environmental conditions and human health)*	• Impacts on climate and air quality: GHG emissions, carbon footprint of priority materials, air emissions • Impacts on water and soil quality: pollutant discharges to water from material extraction & processing; soil contamination due to material extraction & processing and end-of-life management • Impacts on biodiversity: land and habitats • Impacts on human health: population exposure to air and water pollution, related health effects; exposure to risks from waste management and production sites
Responses and actions (policies, measures, framework conditions)	**Support circular use of materials, promote recycling markets and optimise design**	• Taxes, tax reliefs, transfers, regulations supporting circular business models and the use of repaired, refurbished, remanufactured goods • Reform of subsidies encouraging unsustainable use or extraction of materials • Circular Public Procurement; Green Public Procurement; Extended producer responsibility, Deposit-refund, Pay-as-You-Throw schemes • Design for extended lifespans, for recycling & dismantling • Taxes on materials/products raising particular concerns • Bans/guidelines on substances that restrict recycling
	Improve the efficiency of waste management and close leakage pathways	• Investments in waste management • Waste prevention and anti-littering instruments • Bans, taxes on frequently littered items (e.g. plastics) • Bans, taxes on landfilling, on incineration w/o energy recovery
	Boost innovation & orient technological change for more circular material lifecycles	• CE R&D budgets of governments and businesses • Development and international diffusion of CE technologies
	Target setting and planning	• Targets on: resource productivity, recycling, recycled content, waste reduction& prevention, landfilling • CE plans and strategies
	Strengthen financial flows for a circular economy and reduced leakage	• Domestic flows: Government & business expenditure on CE activities; government budgets allocated to CE objectives (link to green budgeting) • International flows: CE related Official Development Assistance (ODA); Foreign Direct Investment (FDI)
	Inform, educate, train	• Product & packaging instruments: eco-labelling, certification schemes, ... • Integration of CE issues in school curriculae & prof. training • Other information and communication instruments
Socio-economic opportunities for a just transition (economic efficiency and social equity)	**Market developments and new business models**	• CE entrepreneurship, goods and services; business models, start-ups, industrial ecology/symbiosis initiatives • Employment markets and jobs; Recycling markets
	Trade developments	• Trade in CE related goods and services • Supply security/autonomy/resilience
	Skills, awareness and behaviour	• CE literacy and skills • Public opinion on CE issues • Behavioural changes (households, consumers, firms)
	Inclusiveness of the transition *(distributional aspects of CE policies)*	To be defined; to reflect how different territories and population groups are affected or benefit from CE policies and actions (young people, women, vulnerable communities, etc.).

Notes

[1] Renewable natural assets also include water from renewable resources. See also section 3.1.

[2] About half of all GHG emissions are estimated to be related to materials management activities (OECD, 2019[2]), and more than 90% of land- and water-related impacts are estimated to be related to resource extraction and processing (International Resource Panel, 2019[11]).

[3] The way trade interacts with material flows creates opportunities or obstacles for a CE.

[4] Material autonomy can in some countries be an important driver for moving towards a CE. A CE can create opportunities for reducing reliance on external markets and increasing the resilience to imports of critical raw materials, which is especially of concern for resource importing countries.

4 The indicator set

4.1. Identifying relevant indicators

The indicators that best reflect major trends related to the transition towards a CE are to be carefully selected. The number of potentially useful indicators can be large. It is therefore necessary to agree upon criteria that guide and validate their choice and keep the selection at a manageable level. Building on earlier OECD work on environmental and green growth indicators the key principles in selecting indicators include: policy relevance and utility for users, analytical soundness, measurability (Box 4.1). These criteria are in line with the indicator selection criteria recommended under the Bellagio principles (EEA, 2021[13]): Relevant, Accepted, Credible, Easy to monitor, and Robust (RACER).

Box 4.1. Key principles in selecting indicators to monitor progress towards a circular economy

Policy relevance and utility for users	The indicator set should have a clear policy relevance, and in particular: • provide a balanced coverage of the key features of a CE with a focus on those that are of common interest to OECD member and partner countries; • be easy to interpret and transparent, i.e. users should be able to assess the significance of the values associated with the indicators and their changes over time; • provide a basis for comparisons across countries; and • lend itself to being adapted to different national contexts and analysed at different levels of detail or aggregation.
Analytical soundness	The indicators should be analytically sound and benefit from a consensus about their validity. They should further lend themselves to being linked to economic and environmental modelling and forecasting.
Measurability	The indicators should be based on data that are available or that can be made available at a reasonable cost, and that are of known quality and regularly updated.

Note: These principles and criteria describe the "ideal" indicator; not all of them will be met in practice. They are in line with the criteria recommended under the Bellagio principles (EEA, 2021[13]).
Source: Adapted from (OECD, 2011[14]) and from (OECD, 1993[15]).

As the CE is a cross-cutting multi-dimensional concept based on systemic approaches, it is important that the indicators selected under the different building blocks and themes:

- are aligned and can be interconnected to inform the assessment of policy outcomes and progress made. Indicators listed under "material life-cycle" could have a counterpart under "responses and actions", as well as under "socio-economic opportunities". This would help linking responses to results obtained as a first step in monitoring the effectiveness of policies.
- fit into an overall narrative framework while supporting more granular analysis.

As information on a CE is not yet available for all dimensions and aspects to be considered, the proposed indicator set encompasses both operational and aspirational indicators.

- *Operational indicators* are indicators that are available or could be made available at a reasonable cost in the short to medium term, and that build on recognised definitions and methodologies.
- *Aspirational indicators* are new or improved indicators that while relevant and desirable to fill gaps require important statistical and methodological efforts to become operational. Such indicators could become part of an internationally coordinated research agenda (see Chapter 5 and 6).

4.2. A 3-tier structure of indicator types

As for other OECD environmental indicators, a 3-tier structure of core, complementary and contextual indicators is used, based on their relevance, measurability, and usefulness to track key features of a CE transition.

- *Core indicators* (or their proxy when the core indicator is currently not measurable) are indicators that capture key elements of a CE, respond to main CE policy questions and point at developments or changes that require further analysis and possible action. Core indicators are designed to provide the big picture of the transition to a CE. They represent a common minimum set of indicators for use in OECD and other international work and that countries would be encouraged to produce or adapt to their own circumstances. The number of core indicators (or their proxy) should be limited so as to facilitate the monitoring and communication of major trends; it should not exceed 20-25.

  Both operational and aspirational core indicators are proposed. Operational core indicators are indicators that are highly relevant from a CE point of view, already measurable in a representative number of OECD countries or that OECD countries would be willing and able to report to in the short term or the medium term (e.g., within the next few years). Operational indicators mainly cover basic waste management, material flow and resource efficiency aspects. Aspirational core indicators are indicators that are highly relevant from a CE point of view, but not yet measurable, and that require further methodological and statistical developments. Most indicators needed to reflect the circularity of materials flows are aspirational, as are many response and opportunity indicators. They are included as an incentive for countries to develop underlying methodologies and/or to produce the required data. They are also proposed to become part of a research roadmap to be internationally coordinated.

  In the future, a *shortlist of core indicators* could be identified as headline indicators to inform high-level decision-makers and civil society and enable wider communication with the public.
- *Complementary indicators*: Indicators that accompany or complement the message conveyed by "core" indicators, by providing additional detail (sub-national detail, sectoral detail) or focus (particular materials or activities), or by covering additional aspects. For country application of the framework, other country-specific indicators can be added. For application in international work, complementary indicators that describe country-specific features are useful for country projects and peer reviews. Complementary indicators also include new and innovative indicators that are yet to be defined and developed, and that could become core indicators in future.
- *Contextual indicators*: indicators that provide background information on socio-economic and environmental variables to facilitate interpretation in the appropriate country context and to inform about drivers of material use. They include general indicators on the characteristics of economic growth (GDP, income), changes in countries' industrial structure, demographic structure and final consumption expenditure, as well as general inequality indicators. They also include general indicators on the factors that influence the environmental implications of material use such as energy and water use or the extent of protected areas.

The indicators are accompanied with references to additional information needed to guide interpretation, and with cross-references to other indicators and indicator sets.

4.3. Proposed indicator set

The list of proposed indicators draws on indicators available from the OECD's own work and work by other international organisations, including:

- The OECD Core Set of Environmental Indicators, OECD sectoral sets of environmental indicators, the set of Green Growth indicators, and OECD indicators to monitor material flows and resource productivity [ENV/EPOC/WPEI(2011)4/REV].
- The revised EU monitoring framework for the circular economy (European Commission, 2023[16]).
- The list of indicators shortlisted by the UNECE Task Force on Measuring Circular Economy.

The list also considers indicators listed in national work, the OECD Inventory of Circular Economy Indicators (OECD, 2020[17]), the work by PACE on Circular Indicators for Governments (PACE, 2021[18]), and work by ISO 59004 WD2 on Circularity Measurement Taxonomy (ISO, 2024[19]). Coherence with the global list of SDG indicators and with the Bellagio principles (EEA, 2021[13]) is ensured. See Annex B for examples of national indicator sets considered.

It should be noted that the indicator set mainly focuses on the national and macro level but can easily be applied or adapted to other levels (sub-national, sectors, industries or firms, products). Furthermore, not all elements of a CE lend themselves to being measured by quantitative indicators and for several aspects current data availability is low. Also, there is no one-to-one correspondence between the CE dimensions and the indicators identified: *a specific indicator can be relevant for more than one CE dimension*; and an indicator listed under one theme can reflect a driver or a pressure for another theme.

Table 4.1 gives an overview of the proposed core indicators, structured in line with the conceptual framework. The list should not be considered as final. It may be reviewed and refined as data availability and quality progress and feedback from the use of the indicators is received.

Table 4.2 presents the complete list of the proposed indicator set together with an initial assessment of their relevance and measurability. Annex A provides further details to this list, including references to other sets in which the proposed indicators feature, and comments on their definitions, interpretation and measurability. This list and its initial assessment will be refined as work on the calculation methods and underlying data sources progresses. New data sources need to be identified for highly relevant indicators that are not yet measurable. Indicators that should be given priority for further research and development need to be identified (see Chapters 5 and 6).

Countries interested in applying the proposed indicator set may adapt it to their own circumstances and policy needs with a phased implementation that takes into account their capacity to engage in the production of CE data and indicators and to ensure proper interpretation (Section 5.2).

4.4. Communicating the indicators

The indicators can be presented and communicated in various ways. The most appropriate way depends on the target audience and on the context in which the indicators are to be used. The joint presentation of a suite of indicators reflecting various dimensions of a CE is most useful. Individual indicators can provide information about specific aspects relevant to the CE transition, but it is the indicator set that ensures a comprehensive and coherent monitoring.

As for other indicators, it is important to note that while CE indicators simplify the communication process, their relevance can vary by country, by audience, and by context. Supplementary information and analyses, and policy-oriented *interpretation* are required for them to acquire their full meaning. The dissemination and communication of the indicators can thus be greatly enhanced by preparing regular synthesis reports or factsheets that would leverage the analyses carried out and by providing links to more detailed statistics and additional information to ensure appropriate context on what is behind the values of the more aggregated indicators. Other tools that could usefully complement the indicators include scenario modelling that could help guide decision-makers towards optimal outcomes, life-cycle assessments (LCA) and environmentally extended input-output analysis that could enrich the messages conveyed by macro-level indicators.

An interesting avenue is to *link and combine different indicators* to balance the message conveyed, reflect the multi-dimensional features of a CE and facilitate interpretation. As a rule, indicators on responses and actions should lend themselves to being related to indicators on the material life cycle and to indicators on opportunities to help linking responses to results obtained as a first step in monitoring the effectiveness of policies. Indicators on the material life cycle should lend themselves to being linked to reference values (benchmarks, thresholds, baselines, objectives, targets) and to environmental issues such as climate change, toxic contamination, biodiversity, natural resource management.

Where data are available, indicators on the material life cycle *broken down by industry* can be presented as part of sector profiles together with data from the SNA and the sequence of SEEA accounts, such as economic activity data (e.g. industry output, value added, operating surplus, employment), information on economic instruments (e.g. taxes, subsidies) and data on environmental pressures (e.g. GHG emissions, use of water resources).

Table 4.1. Overview of framework themes and proposed core indicators

Framework	Themes		Proposed core indicators [a]
Material life-cycle and value chain	The material basis of the economy	1	**Material consumption & productivity** (DMC, RMC): trends and mix
	The circularity of material flows and the management efficiency of materials & waste	2	**Total waste generation:** trends, intensity per GDP and per capita
		3	**Circular material use rate**
		4	**National recycling rate**
		5	**Waste going to final disposal**
	Interactions with trade		none
Interactions with the environment [b]	Natural resource implications	6	**Natural resource index**: energy & mineral resources
		7	**Intensity of use of renewable freshwater resources**
	Environmental quality implications	8	**GHG emissions from production activities**
		9	**Pollutant discharges from production activities to water bodies and proportion safely treated**
		10	**Placeholder: Impacts on human health**
Responses and actions	Support circular use of materials, promote recycling markets and optimise design	11	**Taxes and government support for circular business models**
	Improve the efficiency of waste management and close leakage pathways	12	**Investment in waste management infrastructure, waste collection and sorting** (government, businesses)
	Boost innovation and orient technological change for more circular material lifecycles	13	**R&D expenditure on CE technologies** (government, businesses)
	Target setting and planning		none
	Strengthen financial flows for a circular economy and reduced leakage	14	**Business investment in CE activities**
	Inform, educate, train	15	**Placeholder: Education and training**
Socio-economic opportunities for a just transition	Market developments and new business models	16	**Gross value added of CE sectors**
		17	**Jobs in CE sectors**
	Trade developments		none
	Skills, awareness, behaviour	18	**Placeholder: Behaviour**
	Inclusiveness of the transition	19	**Placeholder:** **Distributional aspects & socio-economic inequality of CE policies**

Notes:

(a) The proposed core indicators include both operational core indicators that are measurable for most OECD countries, and aspirational core indicators that require further work and that countries are encouraged to produce. Placeholders refer to indicators that are yet to be identified and defined. Other indicators that could become core indicators in future can be found in Table 4.2.

(b) Can easily be complemented with other core environmental indicators to give a balanced picture of interactions with the environment. See the OECD Core Set of Environmental Indicators and environmental indicators used to monitor the SDGs.

Table 4.2. Framework themes and proposed indicators

Annex A provides further details to this list, including references to other sets in which the proposed indicators feature, and comments on their definitions, interpretation and measurability.

Framework themes and indicator topics	Proposed indicators (a)	Type (b)	Rel. (c)	Meas. (d)
Material life-cycle and value chain				
1. The material basis of the economy - Production, consumption, accumulation				
1.1 Material inputs	o Direct material inputs (DMI, RMI): trends and mix	Comp	H	H/M
	o Proportion of materials from renewable natural stocks in DMI	Comp	H	H
1.2 Material consumption	**Material consumption and productivity** (DMC, RMC): trends and mix	Core	H	H/M
	o Proportion of materials from renewable natural stocks in DMC	Comp	H	H
	o Proportion of recyclable raw materials in DMC	Comp	M	L
1.3 Material accumulation	o Net addition to stocks	Comp	H	M
	o Changes in man-made stocks of mineral resources	Comp	M	L
2. The circularity of material flows and the management efficiency of materials and waste				
2.1 Waste generation (materials ending up as waste)	**Total waste generation:** trends and intensity per GDP, per capita	Core	H	M
	- Municipal waste generation		M	H/M
	o Waste generation trends by source, and by waste or material type, e.g. Hazardous waste; Waste electrical and electronic equipment; packaging waste, plastics; construction & demolition waste; mining and quarrying waste	Comp	H	M
	o Total primary waste supply by sector *(from waste accounts)*	Comp	H	M/L
	o Waste generation compared to DMC (or DMI) (total, by type of material)	Comp	M	M
	o Food waste generated: Food loss index; Food waste index	Comp	H	L
	o Hazardous waste generated & % treated, by type of treatment	Comp	M	M
2.2 Circularity of material flows	**Circular material use rate**	Core	H	H/M
	o Intermediate consumption of secondary (raw) materials in production processes	Comp	H	L
	o Renewable content of material inputs into production processes	Comp	H	L
2.3 Products diverted from the waste stream	o Ratio of products repaired or reused to new products sold, by product type	Comp	H	M/L
	o Placeholder: Remanufacturing by sector or by branch	Comp	H	
2.4 Materials diverted from final disposal through recycling or recovery	**National recycling rate**	Core	H	M
	- Municipal waste recycling rate			
	o Recycling or recovery rates for selected waste or material types	Comp	H	M
	o Incineration with energy recovery	Comp	M	H
	o Capacity of waste recovery infrastructure, by type	Comp	M	M
2.5 Materials leaving the economic cycle	**Waste going to final disposal**	Core	H	H/L
3. Interactions with trade *(see also "opportunities" below)*				
3.1 Trade in materials	o Material exports, material imports and Physical trade balance (incl. in RMe)	Comp	M	H
	o Material intensity of trade flows (trade value indicator)	Comp	M	H
3.2 Trade in CE related materials and products	o Trade in waste, secondary materials, secondary raw materials, second-hand goods, end-of-life products	Comp	M	M
Interactions with the environment *(to be supplemented with other environmental indicators as appropriate)*				
1. Natural resource implications				
1.1 Changes in natural resource stocks	**Natural resource index:** energy & mineral resources / **Depletion ratios**	Core	M	M/L
	o Domestic extraction from natural stocks (renewable & non-renewable) (trends; mix)	Comp	M	H
	o Changes in natural stocks (global) of mineral resources	Ctx	M	M
	Intensity of use of renewable freshwater resources (water stress)	Core	H	M
	o Intensity of use of forest resources	Comp	H	M
1.2 Other natural resource impacts	o Water abstracted for material extraction and processing	Comp	M	M
	o Water footprint of selected products or sectors	Comp	M	M
	o Natural resource residuals: Unused extraction (by material group)	Comp	M	L

Framework themes and indicator topics	Proposed indicators (a)	Type (b)	Rel. (c)	Meas. (d)
2. Environmental quality implications				
2.1 Impacts on climate	**GHG emissions from production activities** - Total GHG emissions	Core	H	M H
	o Proportion of emissions from waste management or waste sector	Comp	M	M
	o Carbon footprint (CO_2)	Comp	H	M
	o Carbon footprint of priority materials or products, of selected sectors	Comp	M	L
2.2 Impacts on air quality	o Air pollutant emissions from production activities (trends, intensities)	Comp	M	M
2.3 Impacts on water and soil quality	**Pollutant discharges from production activities to water bodies & proportion safely treated** - Total discharges to water bodies & proportion safely treated	Core	H	M
	o Proportion of waste improperly managed (proxy for waste leakage) o Number of uncontrolled open landfills	Comp	M	M
	Placeholder: Soil contamination	Comp	M	
2.4 Impacts on biodiversity	Placeholders: Impacts on land, habitats and species	Comp	H	
2.5 Impacts on human health	**Placeholder**	Core	H	
	Population exposure to air pollution; related premature deaths and welfare costs	Comp	M	M
	Placeholder: Water-related health impacts	Comp	M	
	Placeholder: Population living in the vicinity of waste management sites and production sites	Comp	M	
Responses and actions				
1. Support circular use of materials, promote recycling markets and optimise design				
1.1 Measures supporting circular business models and encouraging reuse, repair, remanufacturing	**Taxes and government support for circular business models** - VAT relief and tax credits for refurbished/repaired items; Tax benefits for businesses for the purchase/use of repaired, refurbished, remanufactured items - Trade tariffs: Import/export taxes for re-used & refurbished equipment compared to taxes on new equipment - Subsidies and other transfers supporting a CE	Core	H	M
	o Circular Public Procurement (CPP) or Green Public procurement (GPP)	Comp	H	L
	o Investments in infrastructure supporting circular business models, beyond waste management	Comp	H	L
	o Population with access to circularity options (e.g. repair services)	Ctx	H	L
1.2 Measures encouraging eco-design	o Design for extending lifespans (i.e. durability, repairability, upgradeability): Requirements for (i) minimum lifespan, warranties, software upgrades; (ii) accessibility to spare parts	Comp	H	M
	o Design for recycling, dismantling & material circularity: (i) Bans/Guidelines on hazardous substances; (ii) Taxes on difficult-to-recycle items; (iii) Availability of guidance documents on design for recycling	Comp	H	M
1.3 Measures encouraging efficient use of materials and economically efficient waste recovery	o Reform of subsidies encouraging unsustainable use or extraction of materials	Comp	H	M
	o Extended Producer Responsibility (EPR) schemes: availability and distance between reported performance and set target	Comp	M	M
	o Availability of Deposit-refund systems (DRS) & Pay-as-you-throw (PAYT) schemes	Comp	M	H/M
2. Improve the efficiency of waste management and close leakage pathways				
2.1 Measures to improve waste management	**Investments in waste management infrastructure, waste collection and sorting**	Core	H	M
	o Population with access to waste management services	Ctx	M	H
2.2. Measures to encourage waste reduction	o Bans, taxes on frequently littered items or single-use items (e.g. plastics)	Comp	H	H
	o Tax rate/tonne landfilled or incinerated	Comp	H	H
	o Landfill bans	Comp	H	H
3. Boost innovation and orient technological change				
3.1 Measures supporting R&D	**R&D expenditure on CE technologies**	Core	H	M/L
3.2 Technology development and international diffusion	o Patented inventions for (1) recycling and secondary raw materials; (2) reuse and repair models	Comp	M	M/L
4. Target setting and planning				
4.1 Targets & distance to targets	Placeholder: Distance to targets (resource productivity; recycling; waste reduction & prevention; recycled content; reuse; landfill)	Comp	H/M	
4.2 CE strategies & plans	Placeholder	Comp	M	

Framework themes and indicator topics	Proposed indicators (a)	Type (b)	Rel. (c)	Meas. (d)
5. Strengthen financial flows				
5.1 Domestic financial flows	**Business investment in CE activities**	Core	H	M
	o Revenue from CE related taxes	Comp	H	H/M
	o Government budgets allocated to CE objectives	Comp	H	M
5.2 International financial flows	o CE related Official Development Assistance (ODA)	Comp	M	L
	o CE related Foreign Direct Investment (FDI)	Comp	M	L
6. Inform, educate and train				
6.1 Information instruments	Placeholders: Eco-labelling; product labelling & certificates; requirement to provide repair guidelines: (i) information on expected lifespan, (ii) dismantling guidelines & material content lists	Comp	M	
6.2 Education and training	**Placeholder: Integration of CE issues in school curricula and professional training**	Core	H	
Socio-economic opportunities for a just transition				
1. Market developments and new business models				
1.1 CE entrepreneurship, goods & services	**Gross value added of CE sectors**	Core	H	H/L
	CE start-ups and trademarks; CE certification of companies	Comp	M	L
1.2 Employment markets & jobs	**Jobs in CE sectors**	Core	H	H/L
	Jobs in sharing economy, reuse and repair activities	Comp	H	L
1.3 Recycling markets	Markets for recycled materials	Comp	H	L
2. Trade developments				
2.1 Trade in CE related goods and services	o Trade in (i) recovered (secondary) and (ii) recycled (secondary raw) materials	Comp	M	M/L
	o Trade in recyclable raw materials	Comp	M	L
2.2 Supply security	o Domestic material autonomy	Comp	H	H
	o Supply security of "strategic" raw materials	Comp	H	M
	o Food security; Energy security	Comp	H	M
3. Skills, awareness and behaviour				
3.1 Skills	Placeholders: CE literacy ; CE skills	Comp	H	
3.2 Awareness	o Public opinion on CE issues and actions	Comp	M	L
3.3 Behaviour	**Placeholder: Change in household, consumer, firm behaviour**	Core	H	
4. Inclusiveness of the transition				
	Placeholder: Distributional aspects & socio-economic inequality of CE policies	Core	M	
Socio-economic and environmental context				
1. Factors that drive demand for materials				
1.1 Socio-demographic factors	o Population growth and structure o Household size	Ctx	M	H
1.2 Economic factors	o GDP growth and structure (trends, value added by sector)	Ctx	M	H
	o Income levels: GDP per capita	Ctx	M	H
	o Income inequality (Gini index); wealth inequality	Ctx	M	H/M
	o Human development index (HDI)	Ctx	M	H
	o Final consumption expenditure: government, household	Ctx	M	H
1.3 Sectoral drivers	o Construction e.g., floor space per capita, value added of construction sector	Ctx	H	M/L
	o Other			
2. Factors that influence the environmental implications of material use				
2.1 Environmental drivers	o Energy supply and consumption: trends and intensities	Ctx	H	H
	o Water use efficiency in production activities and in final consumption	Ctx	H	M
	o Protected areas	Ctx	M	H/M
	o Other			

Notes: (a) All indicators are expected to reflect change over time. For a more detailed list of indicators with references to international indicators' sets and comments on the indicators' measurability and interpretation, see Annex A.

(b) Indicator types: A 3-tier structure, based on the indicators' relevance, measurability and usefulness to track aspects of a circular economy transition: Core indicator (Core) (red colour) or their proxies (-); Complementary indicator (Comp); Contextual indicator (Ctx). Placeholders refer to indicators that are yet to be identified and defined.

(c) Relevance indicates the level of relevance/usefulness of the proposed indicator for the given topic: High (H); Medium (M); Low, to be reviewed (L).

(d) Measurability indicates the current availability of data and agreed methodologies.

High (H) = measurable in the short term; Medium (M) = measurable in the medium term; Low (L) = measurable in the longer term.

5 Measurement and data sources

5.1. Major measurement issues and data gaps

The assessment of the measurability of the indicators proposed in Chapter 4 reveals important gaps in the data required for calculating these indicators. The measurement challenges can be broadly grouped into two categories:

- *Indicator definition*: challenges related to indicator definitions, classifications, measurement boundaries and calculation methods.
- *Data availability and quality*: challenges related to data availability and production, i.e. data are not or hardly available, data are available in formats or levels of detail that are not appropriate, or the data available are of insufficient quality in terms of completeness, coherence (over time, across countries), timeliness, documentation. Data can also be available, but access is hindered by legal or financial constraints (e.g. business confidentiality).

For many core indicators, more than one challenge is experienced. The feasibility for solutions to overcome these challenges also varies among the indicators. A key question is to what extent existing data provide a reliable evidence base for analysing CE policies and their impact on the environment, the economy and well-being.

5.1.1. Indicator definition: Measurement boundaries and classifications

Ideally, the measurement scope of the main indicators selected under the different building blocks and themes should be harmonised so that the indicators can be interconnected. As specified in Chapter 3 indicators listed under "material life-cycle" should have a counterpart under "responses and actions" as well as under "socio-economic opportunities" to help link responses to results obtained as a first step in monitoring the effectiveness of policies. However, the calculation methods and measurement boundaries of several indicators are not yet well defined. This concerns many response and opportunity indicators, as well as several material cycle and environmental quality indicators. The data needed to calculate these indicators are often produced for other purposes than the CE transition and structured according to classifications that are generally not well suited to reflect the multi-dimensional, cross-cutting nature of a circular economy. Approximations are therefore needed to calculate the indicators in the short term.

One of the difficulties lies in identifying the activities, actions and products that contribute to a CE and that can be measured in statistical terms. Current ***statistical classifications*** for activities and products can help but are of limited use. CE activities are not easily delineated and typically integrated in many different activities. The same applies to products. Using existing activity and product classifications thus requires specific guidance. More work is also needed to adapt existing classifications to the needs of multi-purpose and multi-dimensional monitoring. Recent and ongoing revisions of international statistical classifications such as the International Standard Industrial Classification (ISIC) and the Classification of the Functions of Government (COFOG), are first steps in this direction, as is the adoption of the Classification of Environmental Purposes (CEP) that builds upon the Classification of Environmental Protection Activities and Expenditure (CEPA) and the Classification of Resource Management Activities (CReMA).[1]

5.1.2. Data availability and quality

Tracking and reporting progress towards a CE requires data from many different sources that are typically scattered across data providers and holders. These include different ministries and their agencies, NSOs, environmental NGOs, business associations, consumer associations, or research institutes. Relevant data are also available from international sources that countries can use to get started and to fill gaps in national data. Having a good knowledge of available data sources is essential for establishing cost-efficient data collection processes with adequate institutional and data governance arrangements.

In terms of *data availability*, indicators on material flows, waste, recycling and emissions are measurable and in reach for any country given dedicated investments. Indicators on specific features of a CE, like higher R-strategies and activities that maintain the value of products and materials for longer, the circularity of material flows, upstream materials management, life-cycle-wide impacts and costs, are more difficult to measure and require more research and longer-term efforts. The same applies to indicators on the socio-economic, financial and policy aspects of a CE. Other aspects cannot easily be measured in statistical terms and may need to be monitored by using more qualitative types of information.

In terms of *data quality*, a few general challenges exist, which hamper the effective implementation of the indicators. One of these challenges lies with the absence of coherent time series over longer periods that make it difficult to monitor the effects or earlier policies. A second general challenge lies with the lack of data that can easily be combined and interconnected to inform the assessment of policy outcomes and of progress made. A third general challenge lies with the lack of sufficiently granular data to measure how businesses and individuals contribute to the transition to a CE.

The following sub-sections discuss a few data challenges specific to the different building blocks of the CE monitoring framework.

Data on waste

All OECD countries and many other countries in the world produce *data on waste*, but many gaps and data quality issues remain. Common challenges revolve around the following:

- Gaps in data on non-hazardous industrial waste and on the various categories of hazardous waste.
- Gaps in data on the amounts of specific waste streams and related recovery and recycling rates.
- Gaps in data on waste generation and materials management in business sectors and industries. In many countries official data on waste and materials management in the business sector remain scarce, and little information exists on waste prevention measures and the use of secondary raw materials in production processes.
- Frequent changes in definitions and methodologies that reduce the length and the coherence of the time series available and make it difficult to monitor the effects of earlier policy measures.
- Gaps in data documentation (contextual information on waste collection methods, waste prevention measures, national laws and regulations, targets) and in standardised metadata (definitions, surveying methods, breaks in time series) that hamper international harmonisation and coherence over time.

Data on material flows

Material flow data and accounts are produced by all European Union countries and several other OECD countries and are available from international sources (UNEP-IRP, OECD, Eurostat). However, the information available is currently not sufficient to effectively support resource efficiency and circular economy policies. There are important data gaps across countries, sectors and material types that make it difficult to get the full picture of materials use and related environmental impacts. Methodological differences also remain, for example concerning the calculation of demand-based raw material consumption indicators on which international work continues.

In countries where material flow accounts are produced, their usefulness for CE policies is often limited by their focus on economy-wide flows. These accounts do not have a breakdown by economic activity and industry, and do not distinguish between primary and secondary raw materials. This hampers their combination with data on waste or emissions, with product and trade statistics and with economic data from national accounts.

Important gaps include:[2]

- Information on flows of *materials that are important to a CE*, distinguishing between primary and secondary raw materials and their physical trade flows. This is important for assessing resource productivity and decoupling trends, and for understanding the economic benefits of a CE.
- Information on *key materials* and substances, including critical raw materials, environmentally harmful substances, substances that play a role in global biogeochemical cycles and materials that raise global concerns as to their production, use and end-of-life management (e.g. plastics; food; materials in electric and electronic goods; packaging materials).
- Information on material flows *within the economy and across economic activity sectors*.
- Information on the different *processing levels* of materials (raw materials, semi-finished products, finished products) that is needed to identify opportunities for improved performance and efficiency gains in production and consumption processes, and along the supply chain.
- Information on the size and value of the *material stocks locked in the economy*, which is needed to understand the potential of urban mines to contribute to future supply and how they relate to virgin stocks, and to establish links with energy and emissions from their operation.

Data on higher R strategies

As per the definition in Chapter 2, a circular economy is an economy, "where the value of materials in the economy is maximised and maintained as long as possible". Indicators describing particular mechanisms or features of a CE, like *higher R-strategies* and activities that maintain the value of products and materials for longer (i.e. waste prevention, reuse and repair activities, design for circularity, circular consumption) are currently only limitedly measurable. Further work and research are needed in a range of areas. These include, but are not limited to, the average life span of products; the intensity with which products are used; the substitutability of certain goods or services with others; the quality of materials that are reintroduced in production processes through recycling; cost savings of waste prevention measures (e.g. avoided food waste expenditure). Mobilising data on these aspects is not an easy task and may require the use of novel data sourcing techniques. With more and more devices being connected to the internet, so-called digital fingerprints could for example potentially help to derive information on the lifespans for certain product groups (see Table 5.4).

Data on interactions with the environment

Several indicators on environmental implications are measurable and can be derived from environmental, green growth and sustainable development indicators and statistics. Their definitions and the underlying data need however to be improved to better adapt them to CE purposes. Some of these developments are in reach for any country given dedicated investments; other developments require longer term efforts.

Further research and statistical efforts are needed to measure:

- *The availability and deterioration of natural resource stocks.* The production of asset accounts is not yet well developed and does not yet enable an effective tracking of natural resource stocks over time. Stocks of non-renewable resources (minerals, oil, natural gas) and forest resources are generally better covered than stocks of water or land resources. The information made available is however not yet comparable across countries. More work is needed to further develop an operational natural resource index and related balance sheets covering all relevant assets.

- The actual *environmental impacts and costs* of material resource use throughout their life-cycle, considering both the domestic and the footprint perspective. The information available to quantify the (potential) impacts and benefits of a CE and sustainable materials management for climate, air and water pollution, land use and biodiversity is insufficient. Material footprint indicators are often seen as proxies for reflecting the environmental impacts of material flows from a demand-based perspective. Some countries produce indicators on the carbon intensity of materials use, others link material flow data to data on environmental pressures through input-output modelling. But reliable and broadly accepted indicators on the qualitative dimension of "resource productivity and a circular economy" and the real environmental costs of resource use (e.g. in terms of climate change and biodiversity) are still missing. In the short term, efforts could focus for example on quantifying reductions in greenhouse gas emissions and freshwater use due to reduced use of material resources and circular material flows.

Data on policy responses and opportunities

Looking beyond waste and material flow data and interactions with the environment, there are other data gaps that limit measurement of the circular economy transition. The indicator set in Chapter 4 features a range of indicators for *responses and actions and socio-economic opportunities* for a just transition with limited measurability.

Though essential for OECD policy work, most of these indicators require further work both in terms of definitions and measurement boundaries and in terms of data availability and quality. Comparability across countries is a challenge, as is a proper and coherent interpretation of many policy response indicators. Countries' policy responses and approaches vary. Depending on policy priorities, a country may choose to use a variety of tools, such as tax incentives, regulatory instruments, compliance and enforcement measures, research and development, investment in education, making it difficult to identify core indicators that are measurable and equally relevant across OECD countries.

Information on *economic and fiscal instruments* used to improve resource productivity and encourage a circular economy is available but insufficient. Data on subsidies for resource extraction and use and data on market-based instruments that create incentives for circular business models are for example all partial. Data for indicators on *economic policy instruments* are available from the OECD database on "Policy Instruments for the Environment" (PINE) that provides a unique source of information on policy instruments relevant to the environment and natural resource management, and from environmental activity accounts (expenditure, tax revenue, subsidies, environmental goods and services) (OECD, n.d.[20]). Input into the database is provided by countries as well as international sources (Eurostat, OECD). Such data need to be further developed and improved and the measurement boundaries for CE purposes clarified.

Socio-economic aspects such as *employment* in circular activities or household and firm *behaviour* are particularly difficult to measure, yet important to monitor for a just transition. Employment data need to be further developed and improved and the measurement boundaries for CE purposes clarified. Mobilising data on firm behaviour will require longer-term efforts and the exploitation of additional data sources.

Other aspects cannot easily be measured in statistical terms and may need to be monitored by using other more *qualitative types of information*. Examples include aspects related to the institutional set-up and governance, policy instruments other than economic instruments such as regulations and standards, partnerships with civil society and businesses, labelling and other information instruments, as well as aspects related to consumer or household behaviour. Information on some of these aspects could be derived from policy work carried out by the OECD such as work on digitalisation, household behaviour and EPR schemes (OECD, 2023[21]; Brown, Laubinger and Börkey, 2023[22]). However, the use of such information in monitoring progress would require deeper analysis, a regular updating process and a further harmonisation of the information gathered. The usefulness of information compiled under the OECD Climate Actions and Policies Measurement Framework (CAPMF) and the Inclusive Forum on Carbon Mitigation Approaches (IFCMA) could also be explored. Other information for example on people's attitudes to adopting emerging business models or other societal innovations that increase circularity can often be better mobilised using openly accessible digital data offered by popular search engines or social media platforms. Combining these data with information from other sources, such as market data, can enable policymakers to judge the potential for further circular economy initiatives and the need for policy action (see Section 5.2).

Table 5.1. Overview of proposed core indicators and their measurement challenges

Framework themes		Proposed core indicators	Data sources and main areas for progress
Material life-cycle and value chain (production and consumption)			
The material basis of the economy	1	**Material consumption & productivity** (DMC, RMC): trends and mix	Source: EWMF Acc. Work to be done: • Implement harmonised method for estimating demand-based material flows (OECD, UNEP, Eurostat) • Build capacity to produce EWMF Acc, PSUT & material-specific flow accounts
The circularity of material flows	2	**Total waste generation:** trends, intensity per GDP and per capita	Source: waste statistics & accounts. Work to be done: • Improve the quality of waste statistics and expand their scope • Encourage the production of waste accounts
	3	**Circular material use rate**	Source: waste statistics & accounts, EWMF Acc, trade statistics. Work to be done: • Improve the quality/availability of waste statistics & accounts • Build capacity in countries to produce EWMF Acc • Broaden scope of the indicator as data availability progresses
	4	**National recycling rate**	Source: waste statistics. Work to be done:
	5	**Waste going to final disposal**	• Improve the quality of waste statistics and expand their scope
Interactions with the environment (b) (environmental effectiveness)			
Natural resource implications	6	**Natural resource index:** energy & mineral resources	Source: SEEA asset accounts, SNA balance sheets. Work to be done: • Review calculation method and expand its scope • Encourage the production of asset accounts & complete national balance sheets
	7	**Intensity of use of renewable freshwater resources**	Source: water statistics & accounts. Work to be done: • Improve the quality and availability of water statistics & accounts • Specify the measurement boundaries
Environmental quality implications	8	**GHG emissions from production activities**	Source: SEEA AE Acc; emission inventories. Work to be done: • Specify the measurement boundaries • Encourage the production of AE Acc
	9	**Pollutant discharges from production activities to water bodies and % safely treated**	Source: water statistics & accounts. Work to be done: • Improve the quality/availability of water statistics & accounts • Specify the measurement boundaries.
	10	<u>Placeholder</u>: **Impacts on human health**	Work to be done: • Identify most relevant health impact and core indicator
Responses and actions (policies, measures, framework conditions)			
Support circular use of materials	11	**Taxes and government support for circular business models**	Source: SEEA Acc (ESST; ERTR), tax databases, policy instruments databases. Work to be done: • Identify most relevant core indicator • Specify the measurement boundaries • Exploit existing data sources and improve their quality
Improve the efficiency of waste management	12	**Investment in waste infrastructure**	Source: SEEA EE Acc. Work to be done: • Improve the quality/availability of SEEA EE Acc
Boost innovation	13	**R&D expenditure on CE technologies**	Source: R&D databases. Work to be done: • Specify the measurement boundaries • Exploit existing data sources and improve their quality
Strengthen financial flows	14	**Business investment in CE activities**	Source: SEEA Acc (EE, EGSS), SNA, structural business statistics. Work to be done: • Specify the measurement boundaries

Framework themes		Proposed core indicators	Data sources and main areas for progress
			• Improve the quality/availability of EE and EGSS Acc & expand their scope • Integrate CE related questions in business surveys
Inform, educate, train	15	**Placeholder: Education and training**	Specify the measurement boundaries • Identify most relevant core indicator
Socio-economic opportunities for a just transition (economic efficiency and social equity)			
Market developments and new business models	16	**Gross value added of CE sectors**	Source: SNA, SEEA EGSS Acc. Work to be done: • Specify the measurement boundaries • Improve the quality and availability of EGSS Acc and expand their scope • Develop practical guidance on how to use SNA data
	17	**Jobs in CE sectors**	Source: SEEA EGSS Acc, labour statistics. Work to be done: • Specify the measurement boundaries • Improve the quality and availability of EGSS Acc and expand their scope
Skills, awareness, behaviour	18	**Placeholder: Behaviour**	Source: opinion polls, household and business surveys. Work to be done: • Specify the measurement boundaries • Identify most relevant core indicator • Integrate CE related questions in polls and surveys • Investigate novel data sources and sourcing techniques
Inclusiveness of the transition	19	**Placeholder: Distributional aspects & socio-economic inequality of CE policies**	Specify the measurement boundaries • Identify most relevant core indicator

Notes: Data sources: SEEA Acc: accounts in line with the System of Environmental-Economic Accounting; EWMF Acc: economy-wide material flow accounts; AE Acc: air emission accounts; EGSS Acc: accounts on the environmental goods and services sector; EPE Acc: environmental protection expenditure accounts; EE Acc: environmental expenditure accounts (environmental protection, resource management; other); ERTR Acc: environmentally related tax revenue accounts; ESST Acc: accounts on environmental subsidies and similar transfers; PSUT: physical supply and use tables; SNA: national accounts.

5.2. Advancing the measurement through a pragmatic, step-wise approach

Given countries different starting positions and statistical capacities, a pragmatic approach and step-wise improvement in monitoring and measurement are needed starting with indicators that draw on easily accessible and well defined data. Countries that are already more advanced should also be encouraged and supported. The experience thus gained will facilitate work in other countries and at international level. International organisations such as the OECD, UNECE and UNEP, and institutions of the European Union (Eurostat, EEA) can assist by providing a forum for sharing good practices, developing harmonised guidance and providing training and capacity building.

Waste and material flow data are arguably of fundamental importance for measuring transitions to a CE and are available or in reach for any country given dedicated investments. Hence waste management information (e.g., waste generation rates, recovery and recycling rates, disposal rates) can be used as a starting point, in particular data on municipal waste whose availability is often best and that still mirrors trends in household consumption expenditure. These data can be complemented with information on specific waste streams (e.g., construction and demolition waste, food waste, plastic waste, hazardous waste) and with material flow data from national or international sources.

This should be accompanied by:

- *Improvements in the quality of waste statistics*, considering level of detail, coverage of waste streams and materials, coherence over time to monitor the effects of earlier policy measures, coherence across countries to facilitate the exchange of experience and good practices, and breakdown by economic activity and industry to enable linkages with economic statistics and accounts.
- *A progressive expansion of the scope of waste statistics* by broadening the reporting boundaries and the information sources used. The aim would be to integrate information from waste producers, not only on waste, but also on material inputs into production and the use of secondary raw

materials in production, with links to production statistics. This could be complemented with information on up-stream and down-stream measures that feature high in the waste hierarchy and in the circularity ladder (waste prevention, including repair and re-use, preparation for re-use etc.).

- *Improvements in material flow accounts*. The development of compatible material flow accounts and work to improve the quality of data on material flows need to be pursued and consolidated beyond economy-wide material flows, as does work on industry-level and material-specific information that helps identify opportunities for improved circularity and performance along the supply chains.

When it comes to integrated policies and management approaches and to circular economy models, the distinction between waste, materials and products is increasingly blurred. Improving waste statistics and material flow data and accounts is thus not sufficient. *What is needed is a combination of data from various sources.*

An important step would be to *link data on waste and materials and to combine them with product and trade statistics and data from national accounts and from environmental accounts*. This would help analyse both the linkages between raw materials use, material flows, waste and recycling and the circularity of these flows, and their interactions with socio-economic developments. The implementation of an accounting framework building on the System of Environmental Economic Accounting (SEEA) could help combine different datasets to analyse the linkages between raw materials use, material flows, waste and recycling and the circularity of these flows. This would require the development of waste accounts with a direct link to material flow accounts. Other links that need to be explored are the links with accounts on the environmental goods and services sector (EGSS), and environmental expenditure and tax revenue accounts, and the links between asset accounts (resource stocks) and material flows.

Particular attention would need to be given to indicators that describe the contribution of economic activities to a CE (resource use, waste and materials management, emissions and discharges), and that can be linked to socio-economic data (value added, employment, expenditure) and to data on policy instruments (taxes, charges, subsidies). This requires a breakdown of the main indicators on the material life cycle and on policy responses by economic activity sector, which would also enable the construction of sectoral country profiles. This should be accompanied with a progressive improvement of data on the socio-economic and financial aspects of a CE.

5.3. Advancing the measurement through better use of existing data and new data sourcing techniques

Whilst measurement issues and data gaps exist for a range of indicators, there are also a range of data sources and tools that can be explored to fill these gaps. For example, the Bellagio Principles actively encourage the exploitation of a wide range of data and information sources, including data from new sources (principle 4) (EEA, 2021[13]). Opportunities to fill current data gaps in CE indicators can be grouped into three categories:

- *Improving existing data sources available in the public domain* to strengthen their use and usefulness for CE monitoring;
- *Exploiting alternative novel data sources that go beyond official statistics* and that are so far not used for CE monitoring; and
- Making use of *innovative sourcing techniques and tools* to generate new data.

The challenge is to make statistical systems more flexible and responsive to the needs of the multi-dimensional and cross-cutting concept of a CE.

5.3.1. Improving existing data sources in the public domain to strengthen their usefulness for CE monitoring

There are a range of data sources and official statistics from international organisations and national administrations that are currently not used for CE monitoring purposes. The reason for this is often either that a robust methodology is lacking to convert available data into a CE indicator, or that data is too patchy and incomplete to provide meaningful information. Examples of such data sources include tax revenue statistics, labour statistics, EPR compliance reports. Useful data can also be obtained by integrating questions of relevance to a resource-efficient and circular economy in existing surveys, such as structural business surveys, household surveys, public opinion polls.

There are opportunities to improve the information base for CE indicators, by (1) developing methodologies that allow to convert existing data into meaningful indicators and (2) by improving the quality of datasets, to enhance their usefulness for CE monitoring. Table 5.2 provides examples of some existing data sources that are available in the public domain and that are currently only exploited to a limited extent for CE monitoring.

Table 5.2. Examples for opportunities to strengthen the usefulness of existing data sources

Data source	Description	Example application	Challenges
Tax revenue data	Tax revenue can provide detailed information on developments in business practices and consumption patterns and complement data on environmentally related tax revenue from the OECD Pine database and SEEA-related tax revenue accounts.	Revenues from circular taxation can provide information on the consequences that this measure had on consumption or business practices.	Necessary to specify the measurement boundaries.
Labour market statistics	Employment data by industry and services can help to inform the developments in socio-economic opportunities and variables of the CE. Can complement data on employment from SEEA accounts on the environmental goods and services sector (EGSS).	A transition to a more circular economy entails a shift from a material-based economy to a service-based economy. Employment data can help to inform indicators such as amount of "circular jobs".	In some sectors NACE codes may not be granular enough to define "circular jobs". Necessary to specify the measurement boundaries.
EPR compliance reporting	Annual reports by Producer responsibility organization provide a wealth of data on covered waste streams. These data find their way so far only partially into official statistics (e.g. recycling rates).	Can inform costs of collection, expenditure on awareness campaigns, as well as more detailed local information on waste generation, composition and recycling rates.	Limited comparability between countries due to different EPR reporting requirements.
OECD EPIC Household Survey	The OECD Household Survey, conducted in 2008, 2011 and 2022. The 2022 survey includes a sample of more than 17,000 households across nine countries (BE, CAN, CHE, ISR, FR, NL, SWE, UK, USA) and assesses household behaviour in four key areas: energy, transport, waste and food consumption.	The chapters on waste practices and food consumption and can provide valuable data on the drivers behind household behaviour	Only a limited country-coverage. Survey so far conducted on an ad hoc basis.
Eurobarometer	Eurobarometer is a collection of cross-country public opinion surveys conducted regularly on behalf of the EU Institutions.		Questions of relevance to a circular economy can be included.
OECD PINE Database	OECD Database on Policy Instruments for the Environment (PINE) provides vast quantitative and qualitative information on environmental policies across OECD countries. PINE is a.o. used to derive data on environmentally related tax revenue.	Can inform indicators in the "responses & actions" domain of the CE conceptual framework.	Data submission is on voluntary basis and not all country data is currently complete. Necessary to specify the measurement boundaries.

Data source	Description	Example application	Challenges
OECD Intellectual Property Database	Patent databases contain bibliographical and legal event data on patenting from a range of industrialised and developing countries.	Patent counts are a common way to measure innovation. A keyword search of textual information of registered patents allows to identify innovation trends on aspects relevant to a CE transition (e.g. plastics recycling technologies) over time and attributed to countries. The OECD Dataset on patents in environment-related technologies uses a search algorithm of >200 000 classification symbols to identify "green" patents	Patent data do not capture low-technology innovations. Patent registrations do not show technological deployment, value and quality of innovations. Patent data refer to inventors, not to patent owners, and may not directly benefit a given country.

Sources: (Laubinger, Lanzi and Chateau, 2020[23]), (OECD, 2023[21]), (OECD, n.d.[20]), (Dussaux and Agrawala, 2022[24]), (OECD, 2017[25])

5.3.2. Exploiting novel data sources that are so far not used for monitoring

Alternative and novel data sources that go beyond official statistics can also be further exploited for CE monitoring. Individual private sector firms and trade associations collect information, that can have the potential to inform certain CE indicators, at least as proxies. Business sector data can also be used to track progress towards a CE in particular industries (such as car manufacturing, construction, forestry).

Intellectual property rights and firms aiming to maintain their competitive advantage often hinder the public use of private sector data for policy monitoring. Data integration systems may allow pathways to overcoming such accessibility challenges, as they allow data providers to remain in control about the type of data that is shared and who is able to access it (Serna-Guerrero et al., 2022[26]).

The European Environment Agency's "Circularity Metrics Lab" (CML) lists novel dataflows that can provide insights for CE monitoring (EEA, 2024[27]). Four thematic modules focus specifically on plastics, waste prevention, product lifespans and textiles. This can provide countries with information and inspiration to explore opportunities of novel data sources for CE monitoring by disseminating best practices and novel approaches.

Table 5.3 lists a selection of examples of some novel data sources that appear promising for CE monitoring.

Table 5.3. Examples of novel data sources that could be further exploited for CE monitoring

Data source	Description	Example application	Challenges
Repair monitor	The alliance of 'repair cafes' maintains a RepairMonitor, that registers the types of products repaired, age of products and common failures and success rates for repair.	Can inform the uptake of repair activities, as well as product-specific information on items commonly brought for repair and/or requiring repair.	Limited data coverage
International Material Data System	The International Material Data System(IMDS) is a global data repository that contains information on materials used by the automotive industry and their suppliers to maintain data for various reporting requirements (national and international standards, laws and regulations).	The database contains extensive information on materials contained in vehicles and can inform sector-specific indicators on material use, recycled content and improve sector-specific environmental footprint indicators.	Currently not openly accessible, intellectual property barriers to overcome
ChemSHERPA	Different "chemical substances in products" (CiP) information systems are in use to comply with the EU RoHS and REACH regulations. ChemSHERPA was developed by the Japan Ministry of Economy, Trade and Industry as a standardised information system and is used by >100 companies.	CiPs can inform the shar of products that contain certain hazardous substances and can thus provide information on the development of environmental impacts of product groups over time.	Currently not openly accessible, intellectual properly barriers to overcome

EU Digital Product Passport	The EU Commission is currently developing Digital Product Passports (DPP), which aim to contain a bevy of information about a specific product and its sustainability. DPP regulation are staggered, with first product groups to be required to comply being batteries (2026), followed by apparel and consumer electronics. 30 product categories will eventually be required.	Digital Product Passport can contain a.o. information on reparability and recyclability, material content and where these materials were sourced, recycled content and detailed supply chain mapping and life cycle environmental impacts.	Data gathering infrastructure will need to be ramped up, data may be patchy in first years.
Building Information Management systems	Building material passports provide detailed information of the material composition of individual building components or of entire buildings.	The buildings and construction sector is the largest user of materials worldwide and improving information on the material stock in the building sector is crucial. The EU H2020 funded project "Buildings as Material Banks" (BAMB) has developed more than 300 material passports for different components and products.	Necessary to have standardized information systems to ensure compatibility and comparability of different data sources.

Sources: (EEA, 2022[28]; IMDS, 2024[29]; RepairMonitor, 2024[30]; Laubinger and Börkey, 2021[31])

5.3.3. Making use of innovative sourcing techniques and tools to generate new data

The increasing digitalisation of many processes in our society is generating vast amounts of new data streams. There are a range of innovative data sourcing techniques and tools that can help to harness these data streams for purposes of CE monitoring. These include data mining tools, such as web-scraping, digital fingerprints, google trends or data gathered through sensors of Internet of Things (IoT) devices (Table 5.4).

Table 5.4. Examples of innovative data sourcing techniques and tools

Data sourcing technique	Description	Example application	Challenges
Web scraping	Web scraping, web harvesting, or web data extraction is a method used for extracting data from internet websites on a large scale.	Number of video uploads and views of self-repair instructions can indicate people's ability to do their own repairs.	Establish a comprehensive and robust list of relevant search terms.
Digital fingerprints	Browser, device or machine fingerprint is information collected about the software and hardware of a remote computing device for the purpose of identification.	Common browser devices are computers, phones or televisions, but more and more devices tend to be connected to the internet, such as washing machines, radiators, cars, hoovers, forming the "Internet of Things". Their fingerprints can provide useful information about e.g. the age distribution and service life of products.	- Different operating systems (e.g. AndroiD, iOS, Windows), leave different fingerprints, impeding comparability. - Difficult to obtain exact geographical locations, statistics will tend to be global. Using websites that are heavily used by one population could provide an imperfect proxy. - Product models can only be linked to a date when placed on the market and not a date of first use, leaving some uncertainty. Yet this upper-end estimate can still provide an informative age distribution.
Google analytics and google trends	Google Trends is a tool that allows to analyse the popularity of search queries across regions, languages and across time.	Search activity for circular business models (e.g. car sharing, upholstery, bicycle repair) can indicate the uptake of these business models.	Search results will not provide market performance data but can illustrate knowledge about and interest in a certain CE activity or concept.
Internet of Things (IoT)	Devices with sensors, processing ability, software and other technologies that connect and exchange data with other devices and systems over the Internet or other communications networks.	- On an operational level, monitoring product activities can help to improve longevity in future designs or provide targeted preventive maintenance. - IoT can enable pay-per-service and leasing business models, but also helps to generate information about the use and uptake of these, linked to demographic or geographic data.	Privacy concerns could inhibit the use of data generated for public monitoring of the CE transition.

Data sourcing technique	Description	Example application	Challenges
Google Street View	A technology that provides interactive panoramas from positions along many streets in the world.	Analysis of Street View images could inform estimates on building materials contained in the housing stock.	Defining a methodology for comprehensive and reliable data mining may be a challenge.

Sources: (EEA, 2022[28]; Raghu et al., 2022[32])

Whilst all of these data sources and data mining methods have their limitations, they can play a useful role in complementing more traditional data collection techniques, such as surveys and official databases and statistics. Despite their drawbacks, there are opportunities for their use to develop proxy indicators where data from official and conventional sources is currently lacking, or about aspects that these official databases do not cover. This report only touches upon some of these opportunities, and there is merit in investigating further and in more detail how these novel data sources and collection techniques can contribute to improving the measurability of the CE indicator set in the future and what role national statistical offices could play.

Notes

[1] The Classification of Environmental Purposes (CEP) was adopted by the UN Statistical Commission at its 55th session in March 2024.

[2] These shortcomings and work areas were identified in the 2021 progress assessment of Adherents' alignment with the OECD Council Recommendation on Resource Productivity [C(2021)62].

6 Towards better information for a resource efficient and circular economy

The shift to a circular economy entails having a new perspective to measure the different components of the economy. This report proposes a conceptual framework and a set of indicators, that, if fully measured, helps to monitor the transition towards a CE with reduced environmental impacts and increased social benefits. Whilst some of the indicators proposed are already measurable, others exist so far largely conceptually and require further research and elaboration to become operational.

The refinement and implementation of the proposed indicator set will require further work in terms of (i) data availability and quality, (ii) indicator definitions and measurement methods, and (iii) indicator interpretation and use. This goes with an enhanced use of accounting frameworks, in particular the System of Environmental Economic Accounting (SEEA), and an in-depth review of international statistical classifications to ensure coherence across data sets and help harmonise the indicators' measurement boundaries. It also goes with a further review of novel data sources and sourcing techniques and the preparation of practical and statistical guidance to improve measurement.

As measuring progress towards a CE has become a very dynamic field with many national and international activities, steered by governments, NGOs, academics and business associations, good international coordination is important to distil good practices and capitalise on all the advances. What is needed is a measurement and indicator research agenda, and a *roadmap* to work towards improving information on a CE in a coordinated way. Such a roadmap would distinguish between adjustments and improvements that can be made in the short- to medium-term, and developments that require further work and research in the longer term.

The 3-tier structure with a distinction between core indicators, complementary indicators and contextual indicators helps identify the data and indicators that should be prioritised. The following lists outline areas and actions that could be given priority and other necessary developments. Some of this further work might be appropriate work for OECD; some of it might best be undertaken by other organisations or institutions, or by countries.

Areas and actions that could be given priority include:

- Continue work to improve the quality and availability of *waste statistics and material flow accounts*.
- Continue work on *linking data on waste and materials*, and combining them with product and trade statistics.
- Further develop *policy response indicators* building on SEEA accounts and the OECD PINE database, leveraging ongoing OECD work including under the Inclusive Forum on Carbon Mitigation Approaches (IFCMA), and exploiting work on digitalisation, household behaviour and EPR schemes for their suitability for deriving selected indicators.
- Continue work on *combining physical and monetary data*, and on linking data on the contribution of economic activities to a circular economy, to socio-economic data and to data on policy instruments. This requires the application of accounting frameworks, including the SEEA, and the

use of coherent statistical classifications. It also requires a review of existing data collections to maximise opportunities for linking different data sets.

- Further specify the *definitions and calculation methods* to be used for core indicators, including their measurement boundaries, related data sources (current, novel) and statistical classifications.
- Develop practical guidance for *mobilising data and statistics* on all dimensions of a CE and implementing a *step-wise approach* to improving measurement in countries and at international level.
- Develop practical guidance on the *use and communication* of CE indicators considering different audiences and countries' specific contexts (e.g. socio-economic, institutional, policy).

Other necessary developments include:

- Research on and statistical development of indicators that reflect *higher R-strategies* and the value of materials across their life cycle, including indicators on material flows within production processes and across industries.
- Work towards optimising and aligning international statistical *classifications* (activities, products) for CE purposes.
- Research on and statistical development of *environmental quality indicators* to better reflect how natural resource use and materials management translate into potential impacts on or benefits for climate, air and water pollution, land use and biodiversity, considering both the domestic and the footprint perspective.
- Further investigation of *novel data sources* and innovative measurement approaches and sourcing techniques (see Chapter 5). Future work could investigate into such opportunities further, whilst also further assessing the challenges and how to overcome these.
- A review of the applicability of the monitoring framework to the *business sector and to specific industries*, also considering ongoing work at ISO (International Organization for Standardization)[1] on a taxonomy for circular economy measurement and on standards and conformity assessments for organisations (ISO, 2024[19]).

Insights from these developments will help further refine and specify the indicator set. They may also help identify a shortlist of core indicators that could be used as headline indicators to inform high-level decision-makers and civil society and enable wider communication with the public.

Note

[1] ISO is an independent, non-governmental international organization with a membership of 170 national standards bodies.

References

Alaerts, L. et al. (2019), "Towards a more direct policy feedback in circular economy monitoring via a societal needs perspective", *Resources, Conservation and Recycling*, Vol. 149, pp. 363-371, https://doi.org/10.1016/j.resconrec.2019.06.004. [52]

Bangert, H. (2020), "Japan's Circularity - A Panorama of Japanese Policy, Innovation, Technology and Industry Contributions Towards Achieving the Paris Agreement", http://www.eu-japan.eu/ (accessed on 9 November 2022). [39]

Brown, A., F. Laubinger and P. Börkey (2023), "New Aspects of EPR: Extending producer responsibility to additional product groups and challenges throughout the product lifecycle", *OECD Environment Working Papers*, No. 225, OECD Publishing, Paris, https://doi.org/10.1787/cfdc1bdc-en. [22]

Circular Flanders (2022), *Circular Economy Monitor Flanders*, https://cemonitor.be/en/home-english/ (accessed on 24 October 2022). [51]

Coulomb, R. et al. (2015), "Critical Minerals Today and in 2030: An Analysis for OECD Countries", *OECD Environment Working Papers*, No. 91, OECD Publishing, Paris, https://doi.org/10.1787/5jrtknwm5hr5-en. [35]

DANE (2022), *Quinto reportte de economía circular*, https://www.dane.gov.co/index.php/estadisticas-por-tema/ambientales/economia-circular (accessed on 24 October 2022). [50]

Dussaux, D. and S. Agrawala (2022), "Quantifying environmentally relevant and circular plastic innovation: Historical trends, current landscape and the role of policy", *OECD Environment Working Papers*, No. 199, OECD Publishing, Paris, https://doi.org/10.1787/1f6dbd07-en. [24]

EASAC (2016), "Indicators for a circular economy", https://easac.eu/fileadmin/PDF_s/reports_statements/Circular_Economy/EASAC_Indicators_web_complete.pdf (accessed on 20 October 2022). [42]

EEA (2024), *Circularity Metrics Lab*, https://www.eea.europa.eu/en/circularity (accessed on 17 May 2024). [27]

EEA (2022), "Monitoring the circular economy using emerging data streams", https://www.eea.europa.eu/publications/monitoring-the-circular-economy-with (accessed on 30 January 2024). [28]

EEA (2021), *The Bellagio Declaration*, https://epanet.eea.europa.eu/reports-letters/reports-and-letters/bellagio-declaration.pdf/view (accessed on 30 January 2024). [13]

European Commission (2024), *Critical raw materials*, https://single-market-economy.ec.europa.eu/sectors/raw-materials/areas-specific-interest/critical-raw-materials_en (accessed on 14 February 2024). [37]

European Commission (2023), *The revised EU monitoring framework for circular economy*, https://eur-lex.europa.eu/legal-content/EN/TXT/?uri=COM%3A2023%3A306%3AFIN&qid=1684143860344 (accessed on 14 February 2024). [16]

European Commission (2018), "A sustainable Bioeconomy for Europe: strengthening the connection between economy, society and the environment", p. 107, https://doi.org/10.2777/478385. [7]

Eurostat (2024), *Contribution of recycled materials to raw materials demand - end-of-life recycling input rates (EOL-RIR) (cei_srm010)*, https://ec.europa.eu/eurostat/cache/metadata/en/cei_srm010_esmsip2.htm (accessed on 16 February 2024). [33]

Eurostat (2024), *Overview - Circular Economy Monitoring Framework*, https://ec.europa.eu/eurostat/web/circular-economy (accessed on 14 February 2024). [55]

Geng, Y. et al. (2012), "Towards a national circular economy indicator system in China: an evaluation and critical analysis", *Journal of Cleaner Production*, Vol. 23/1, pp. 216-224, https://doi.org/10.1016/j.jclepro.2011.07.005. [40]

Graedel, T. et al. (2012), "Methodology of Metal Criticality Determination", *Environmental Science & Technology*, Vol. 46/2, pp. 1063-1070, https://doi.org/10.1021/es203534z. [36]

Hanemaaijer, A. et al. (2021), "Integrale Circulaire Economie Rapportage 2021", https://www.pbl.nl/sites/default/files/downloads/pbl-2021-integrale-circulaire-economie-rapportage-2021-4124.pdf (accessed on 24 October 2022). [47]

IMDS (2024), *IMDS Material Data System - Information Page*, https://public.mdsystem.com/en/web/imds-public-pages/home (accessed on 17 May 2024). [29]

International Resource Panel (2019), "Global Resources Outlook", https://www.resourcepanel.org/reports/global-resources-outlook. [11]

ISO (2024), *ISO/DIS 59004(en), Circular Economy – Terminology, Principles and Guidance for Implementation*, https://www.iso.org/obp/ui/en/#iso:std:iso:59004:dis:ed-1:v1:en (accessed on 14 February 2024). [19]

Laubinger, F. and P. Börkey (2021), "Labelling and Information Schemes for the Circular Economy", *OECD Environment Working Papers*, No. 183, OECD Publishing, Paris, https://doi.org/10.1787/abb32a06-en. [31]

Laubinger, F., E. Lanzi and J. Chateau (2020), "Labour market consequences of a transition to a circular economy: A review paper", *OECD Environment Working Papers*, No. 162, OECD Publishing, Paris, https://doi.org/10.1787/e57a300a-en. [23]

Magnier, C. (2017), "10 Key indicators for Monitoring the Circular Economy", https://www.statistiques.developpement-durable.gouv.fr/sites/default/files/2018-10/datalab-18-economie-circulaire-Edition-2017-anglais.pdf (accessed on 21 October 2022). [45]

Mayer, A. et al. (2018), "Measuring Progress towards a Circular Economy: A Monitoring Framework for Economy-wide Material Loop Closing in the EU28", *Journal of Industrial Ecology*, Vol. 23/1, pp. 62-76, https://doi.org/10.1111/jiec.12809. [53]

McCarthy, A., R. Dellink and R. Bibas (2018), “The Macroeconomics of the Circular Economy Transition: A Critical Review of Modelling Approaches”, *OECD Environment Working Papers*, No. 130, OECD Publishing, Paris, https://doi.org/10.1787/af983f9a-en. [8]

MOEJ (2018), “Fundamental Plan for Establishing a Sound Material-Cycle Society”, https://www.env.go.jp/content/900453386.pdf (accessed on 18 October 2022). [41]

MOEJ (2018), “The 4th Fundamental Plan for Establishing a Sound Material-Cycle Society”, https://www.env.go.jp/recycle/recycle/circul/keikaku/pam4_E.pdf (accessed on 20 October 2022). [38]

MOEJ (2013), “3rd Fundamental Plan for Establishing a Sound Material-Cycle Society”, https://www.env.go.jp/en/recycle/smcs/3rd-f_plan.pdf (accessed on 20 October 2022). [44]

MOEJ (2010), “Establishing a sound material-cycle society”. [43]

Moraga, G. et al. (2019), “Circular economy indicators: What do they measure?”, *Resources, Conservation and Recycling*, Vol. 146, pp. 452-461, https://doi.org/10.1016/j.resconrec.2019.03.045. [54]

OECD (2023), *How Green is Household Behaviour?: Sustainable Choices in a Time of Interlocking Crises*, OECD Studies on Environmental Policy and Household Behaviour, OECD Publishing, Paris, https://doi.org/10.1787/2bbbb663-en. [21]

OECD (2022), *Global Plastics Outlook: Economic Drivers, Environmental Impacts and Policy Options*, OECD Publishing, Paris, https://doi.org/10.1787/de747aef-en. [3]

OECD (2020), *The Circular Economy in Cities and Regions: Synthesis Report*, OECD Urban Studies, OECD Publishing, Paris, https://doi.org/10.1787/10ac6ae4-en. [17]

OECD (2019), *Global Material Resources Outlook to 2060: Economic Drivers and Environmental Consequences*, OECD Publishing, Paris, https://doi.org/10.1787/9789264307452-en. [2]

OECD (2017), *Green Growth Indicators 2017*, OECD Green Growth Studies, OECD Publishing, Paris, https://doi.org/10.1787/9789264268586-en. [25]

OECD (2015), *Material Resources, Productivity and the Environment*, OECD Green Growth Studies, OECD Publishing, Paris, https://doi.org/10.1787/9789264190504-en. [12]

OECD (2011), *Towards Green Growth: Monitoring Progress: OECD Indicators*, OECD Green Growth Studies, OECD Publishing, Paris, https://doi.org/10.1787/9789264111356-en. [14]

OECD (2008), *OECD Recommendation of the Council on Resource Productivity*, https://legalinstruments.oecd.org/en/instruments/OECD-LEGAL-0358 (accessed on 16 February 2024). [4]

OECD (2004), “Towards Waste Prevention Performance Indicators, Part 1, 2 and 3”, https://one.oecd.org/document/env/epoc/wgwpr/se(2004)1/final/en/pdf. [10]

OECD (2000), “Strategic Waste Prevention: OECD Reference Manual”, https://one.oecd.org/document/ENV/EPOC/PPC(2000)5/FINAL/en/pdf. [9]

OECD (1993), “OECD Core Set of indicators for environmental performance reviews”, *Environment Monograph N.83*, https://one.oecd.org/document/OCDE/GD(93)179/En/pdf (accessed on 14 February 2024). [15]

OECD (n.d.), *Policy Instruments for the Environment (PINE) Database*, https://pinedatabase.oecd.org/ (accessed on 28 June 2022). [20]

PACE (2021), "Circular Indicators for Governments", https://pacecircular.org/sites/default/files/2021-04/CircularIndicatorsForGovernments_FINAL.pdf (accessed on 24 October 2022). [18]

PBL (2018), "Circular Economy: what we want to know and can measure", *PBL Netherlands Environmental Assessment Agency*, https://www.pbl.nl/en/publications/circular-economy-what-we-want-to-know-and-can-measure (accessed on 13 February 2024). [6]

Potting, J. et al. (2017), "CIRCULAR ECONOMY: MEASURING INNOVATION IN THE PRODUCT CHAIN Policy Report", https://www.pbl.nl/sites/default/files/downloads/pbl-2016-circular-economy-measuring-innovation-in-product-chains-2544.pdf (accessed on 13 December 2021). [5]

Prins, A. and A. Hanemaaijer (2022), "Voortgangsbericht circulaire economie - 2022", https://www.pbl.nl/sites/default/files/downloads/pbl-2022-voortgangsbericht-circulaire-economie-2022-4470.pdf (accessed on 24 October 2022). [48]

Raghu, D. et al. (2022), "Enabling Component Reuse from Existing Buildings through Machine Learning, Using Google Street View to Enhance Building Databases", *CAADRIA proceedings, Proceedings of the 27th Conference on Computer Aided Architectural Design Research in Asia (CAADRIA) [Volume 2]*, https://doi.org/10.52842/conf.caadria.2022.2.577. [32]

RepairMonitor (2024), *Dashboard RepairMonitor*, https://dashboard.repairmonitor.org/?language=en&cafe=all&country=fr&year=all (accessed on 17 May 2024). [30]

Schreyer, P. and C. Obst (2015), "Towards Complete Balance Sheets in the National Accounts: The case of Mineral and Energy Resources", *OECD Green Growth Papers*, No. 2015/2, OECD Publishing, Paris, https://doi.org/10.1787/5js319256pvf-en. [34]

Scribe, C. et al. (2021), "Key indicators for monitoring the circular economy - 2021 Edition", https://www.statistiques.developpement-durable.gouv.fr/sites/default/files/2021-08/datalab_key_indicators_circular_economy_august2021.pdf (accessed on 18 October 2022). [46]

Serna-Guerrero, R. et al. (2022), "Overcoming data gaps for an efficient circular economy: A case study on the battery materials ecosystem", *Journal of Cleaner Production*, Vol. 374, p. 133984, https://doi.org/10.1016/j.jclepro.2022.133984. [26]

UNECE (2024), *Conference of European Statisticians Guidelines for Measuring Circular Economy - Part A: Conceptual Framework, Indicators and Measurement Framework*, https://unece.org/sites/default/files/2024-02/ECECESSTAT20235_WEB.pdf. [1]

UNECE (2021), *In-depth review of measuring circular economy*, https://unece.org/sites/default/files/2021-05/08_Measuring_Circular_Economy_full_version_ENG.pdf (accessed on 24 October 2022). [49]

Annex A. Proposed indicator set - Detailed list

This Annex presents a detailed list of the proposed indicators with references to international indicator sets that include the same or similar indicators and comments on the indicators' definition, measurability and interpretation.

It will serve as a basis for refining the indicator set in future and specifying the definitions, calculation methods and data sources to be used.

Notes:

(a) All indicators are expected to reflect change over time. Core indicators are in red colour.

(b) **Indicator types**: A 3-tier structure is used based on the indicators' relevance, measurability and usefulness to track aspects of a circular economy transition.

Core indicator (Core); Complementary indicator (Comp); Contextual indicator (Ctx).

- Core indicators (or their proxy when the core indicator is currently not measurable) are indicators that capture key elements of a CE, respond to main CE policy questions and point at developments or changes that require further analysis and possible action. Core indicators are designed to provide the big picture of the transition to a CE. They represent a common minimum set of indicators for use in OECD and other international work and that countries would be encouraged to produce or adapt to their own circumstances. The number of core indicators (or their proxies) should be limited and not exceed 20-25.

  Both operational and aspirational core indicators are proposed. Operational core indicators are indicators that are highly relevant from a CE point of view, already measurable in a representative number of OECD countries or that OECD countries would be willing and able to report to in the short term or the medium term (e.g., within the next few years). Operational indicators mainly cover basic waste management, material flow and resource efficiency aspects. Aspirational core indicators are indicators that are highly relevant from a CE point of view, but not yet measurable, and that require further methodological and statistical developments. Most indicators needed to reflect the circularity of materials flows are aspirational. They are included as an incentive for countries to develop underlying methodologies and/or to produce the required data. They are also proposed to become part of an international measurement agenda and roadmap. A shortlist of core indicators could further be identified as headline indicators to inform high-level decision-makers and civil society and to support wider communication with the public.
- **Complementary indicators**: Indicators that accompany or complement the message conveyed by "core" indicators, by providing additional detail (sub-national detail, sectoral detail) or focus (particular materials or activities), or by covering additional aspects. For country application of the framework, other country-specific indicators can be added. For application in international work, complementary indicators that describe country-specific features are particularly useful for country projects and peer reviews. Complementary indicators also include new and innovative indicators that are yet to be defined and developed, and that could become core indicators in future.
- **Contextual indicators**: indicators that provide background information on socio-economic and environmental variables to facilitate interpretation in the appropriate country context (e.g., GDP, industrial structure, income) and indicators that inform about general drivers of material use and about factors that influence the environmental implications of materials use.

(c) **Relevance** indicates the level of relevance/usefulness of the proposed indicator for the given topic: High (H); Medium (M); Low and to be reviewed (L).

Relevance is assessed with respect to the following criteria:

- ability to provide a representative picture of the material life-cycle, its interactions with the environment, and society's responses.
- simplicity, ease of interpretation
- ability to show trends over time, and responsiveness to changes
- ability to provide a basis for international comparisons;
- existence of a threshold or reference value against which to compare it, so that users can assess the significance of the values associated with it.

(d) **Measurability** indicates the current availability of data and agreed methodologies, except of placeholders.

High (H) = measurable in the short term; basic data available for a majority of OECD members and a few non-members; indicator methodology well defined with consensus about validity.

Medium (M) = measurable in the medium term; the indicator is being developed and should be available in the near future; basic data partially available; goes with further efforts to improve the quality of underlying data (consistency, comparability, timeliness) and their geographical coverage (number of countries covered).

Low (L) = measurable in the longer term; major methodological or data gaps, calling for sustained data collection & conceptual efforts.

(e) **Related indicator sets**: international indicator set that includes the same or a similar indicator.
OECD: set of material flow and resource productivity indicators (MFRP), core set of environmental indicators (CEI), green growth indicators (GGI); EU revised monitoring framework (EU-MF)[1]; SDG global indicator set (SDG); UNECE Working Package 3 (WP3) list.

Table A.1. Framework themes and proposed indicator set: Detailed list

Framework themes and indicator topics	Proposed indicators (a)	Type (b)	Rel. (c)	Meas. (d)	Related indic. sets (e)	Comments
Material life-cycle and value chain *(Production and consumption)*						
1. The material basis of the economy *(level & characteristics of materials supply and their use in the economy)*						
1.1 Material inputs	o Direct material inputs (trends; intensities; mix) a. Production-based domestic material inputs (DMI) b. Demand-based raw material inputs (RMI)	Comp	H	H/M	OECD MFRP; WP3 Core	Double-headed indicator DMI & RMI, with complementary but related messages. Reflects the (raw) material basis of the economy accounting for domestic extraction and imports. To be read with information on the materials mix. DMI and RMI cannot be aggregated at international level without double counting (e.g., EU, OECD regions). Could be a core indicator for use by countries. Intensity and productivity ratios should be calculated using adequate components of GDP.
	o Proportion of materials from renewable natural stocks in DMI	Comp	H	H	OECD MFRP	Links to biological material cycles. Could equally be related to RMI.
1.2 Material consumption	**Material consumption and productivity** (trends; mix) a. Production-based domestic material consumption (DMC) b. Demand-based raw material consumption (RMC) (material footprint) c. Production-based material productivity (GDP/DMC) d. Demand-based raw material productivity (net disposable income/RMC)	Core	H	H/M	SDG 8.4.2/12.2.2 SDG 8.4.1/12 2.1 OECD MFRP, GGI, CEI; EU MF: footprint, productivity; WP3 Core: footprint	Double-headed indicators: DMC & RMC, with complementary but related messages. DMC can be related to future waste, recognising that there is a time lag between material consumption and waste generation. To be read with information on the materials mix. To be complemented with information on unused material flows (see "natural resource implications"). DMC and RMC can be aggregated at international level without double counting (e.g., EU, OECD regions). N.B. work on common international method for demand-based measures is ongoing. Material productivity could be the main core indicator, with DMI/RMI and DMC/RMC being complementary indicators. It characterises the environmental and economic efficiency with which natural resources and materials are used in production and consumption, and informs about the results of policies and measures that promote resource productivity and sustainable materials management in all sectors. Complemented with information on the share of recycled (secondary raw) materials, it informs about the results of policies that promote a circular use of materials. See "circular use rate" below. Measures of material productivity extend productivity measurement and analysis to material resources and complement other single factor productivity measures such as labour productivity and capital productivity. Material intensity indicators could be used in addition to reflect the level of decoupling between material consumption and economic growth. Intensity and productivity ratios should be calculated using adequate components of GDP. In the absence of reliable data on net or gross national income, GDP can be used as a proxy for calculating the demand-based indicator.

Framework themes and indicator topics	Proposed indicators (a)	Type (b)	Rel. (c)	Meas. (d)	Related indic. sets (e)	Comments
	o Proportion of materials from renewable natural stocks in DMC	Comp	H	H	OECD MFRP	Links to biological material cycles. Could equally be related to RMC.
	o Proportion of recyclable raw materials in DMC	Comp	M	L	OECD MFRP	Links to circular design. Requires a common definition of "recyclable" materials. "Recyclability" is challenging to define. Technical and economic factors play a role.
1.3 Material accumulation	o Net addition to stocks	Comp	H	M	OECD MFRP	Reflects the physical growth of the economy. Links to potential future waste and to potential future "urban" mines of raw materials. Requires the further development of material flow accounts.
	o Changes in man-made stocks of mineral resources	Comp	M	L		
2. The circularity of material flows and the management efficiency of materials and waste *(economy-wide; in activity sectors; with reference to R strategies and CE mechanisms)*						
2.1 Waste generation (materials ending up as waste)	**Total waste generation** (trends; intensity per GDP, per capita) – Municipal waste generation	Core	H M	M H/M	OECD CEI; EU MF, SDG 11.6.1; WP3 Core	Waste generation should ideally cover all primary waste generated to be relevant from a macro-economic CE point of view. If not available, municipal waste could be used as a proxy to get started. Municipal waste is a good indicator to reflect efforts or the lack of efforts by citizens and households. Idem for other waste-related indicators proposed here. Waste generation should ideally distinguish between mineral waste and other waste.
	o Waste generation trends by source, and by waste or material type (% contribution to total; trends) – e.g., Hazardous waste; waste electrical and electronic equipment; packaging waste, plastics; construction & demolition waste; mining and quarrying waste	Comp	H	M	OECD CEI; EU MF	Complements the core indicator with a breakdown by source sector (ISIC/NACE) and by type of waste or material. Particular attention could also be given to waste streams that raise concerns such as hazardous waste, WEEE, plastics, packaging waste, C&D waste, mining and quarrying waste. To be related to indicators on targets and distance to targets to monitor policy outcomes.
	o Total primary waste supply by sector *(from waste accounts)* (% contribution to total, intensities per value added)	Comp	H	M/L		Indicator derived from waste accounts building on the SEEA with a breakdown by sector (ISIC/NACE) aligned with national accounts, which opens up additional analyses. Requires the elaboration and maintenance of waste accounts in countries.
	o Waste generation compared to DMC (or DMI): total, by type of material	Comp	M	M	OECD MFRP	Relates total primary waste generation to the amount of material consumed or used in the economy. Could be applied to product groups. Interpretation: Should take into account stocks, recognising that there is a time lag between material consumption and waste generation.
	Food waste generated – Food loss index (production and supply levels) – Food waste index (retail and consumption levels)	Comp	H	L	SDG 12.3.1, EU MF; WP3 Core	Reducing food waste and food loss has an enormous potential for saving the resources used to produce food. Links to environmental implications. Most relevant indicator to be selected. Methodological guidance exists from Eurostat/EU and from SDG indicator metadata (FAO, UNEP).
	o Hazardous waste generated & % treated, by type of treatment	Comp	M	M	SDG 12.4.2	Hazardous waste raises particular management and environmental issues. Links to the implementation of the Basel Convention, OECD decisions and EU Directives.

Framework themes and indicator topics	Proposed indicators (a)	Type (b)	Rel. (c)	Meas. (d)	Related indic. sets (e)	Comments
2.2 Circularity of material flows	**Circular material use rate:** all materials, material groups, selected materials (% contribution of recycled materials (secondary raw materials) to material consumption)	**Core**	H	H/M	EU MF; OECD MFR;P WP3 Core	Links data from waste statistics to data from material flow accounts and trade statistics. Can be calculated in different ways depending on the purpose and the data available. [A] To measure a country's recycling efforts, whether domestically or abroad, it can be calculated as: *recycled amounts* (waste recycled in domestic recovery plants minus imported waste destined for recycling plus exported waste destined for recycling abroad) *over material use* (DMC+recycled amounts). [B] To reflect the extent to which recycled materials contribute to satisfying a country's demand for materials without adding pressure on natural resources, it can be calculated as: *recycled amounts* (waste recycled in domestic recovery plants plus imported waste destined for recycling minus exported waste destined for recycling abroad) *over material use* (DMC+recycled amounts). Should ideally be calculated using amounts of materials coming out of recycling processes, net of losses during the recycling process (cf. Japan). Can also be calculated using the amounts of waste being sent to recycling including losses during the recycling process (cf. Eurostat; Circular material use rate — Calculation method — 2018 edition - Products Manuals and Guidelines - Eurostat (europa.eu)). The use of DMC avoids double counting when aggregating at international level (e.g. across EU, OECD regions). At national level, countries may wish to calculate this indicator by relating the amounts recycled to DMI (see the circular input use rate used in Japan)[1]. Should ideally be calculated using raw material consumption (RMC) when available. Could be expanded to account for reused materials if data availability permits.
	o Intermediate consumption of secondary (raw) materials in production processes (processing and manufacturing)	Comp	H	L	EU MF	Complements the circular material use rate. Level of application (tbd): by sector, material type, product groups or company. Could focus on "strategic" raw materials (see also "supply security" below). Feasibility of a harmonised measurement at international level to be explored. Builds on data from material system analysis. See for example "Contribution of recycled materials to raw materials demand - end-of-life recycling input rates (EOL-RIR) (cei_srm010) (europa.eu)": (Eurostat, 2024[33])
	o Renewable content of material inputs into production processes (average %)	Comp	H	L	ISO WD2 59020; WP3 Core	Relates to material substitution and to biological material cycles. Reflects the proportion of virgin renewable materials in material inputs; to be complemented with indicators on the proportion of recycled and reused content in material inputs. Level of application (tbd): by sector, product groups or company. Feasibility of a harmonised measurement at international level to be explored. Data disclosure by companies to be explored. Interpretation to consider the overall environmental footprint of renewable materials vs. non-renewable materials and the sustainability of the management of the natural resource from which they are extracted.

Framework themes and indicator topics	Proposed indicators (a)	Type (b)	Rel. (c)	Meas. (d)	Related indic. sets (e)	Comments
2.3 Products diverted from the waste stream *(repair, remanufacture, reuse)*	○ Ratio of products repaired or reused to new products sold, by product type	Comp	H	M/L	WP3 Core	Can be related to product design and manufacture. Data availability and alternative data sources to be explored. Feasibility of a harmonised measurement at international level to be explored.
	○ Placeholder: Remanufacturing by sector or by branch	Comp	H			
2.4 Materials diverted from final disposal through recycling or recovery	**National recycling rate**: proportion recycled in total waste generated (or collected) – Municipal waste recycling rate	**Core**	H	M	SDG 12.5.1 ; OECD MFRP, CEI, GGI/ EU MF; WP3 Core	Refers to all waste materials recycled in the country plus quantities exported for recycling out of total waste generated in the country, minus material imported for recycling. Recycling includes material recycling, codigestion/anaerobic digestion and composting/aerobic process if the compost/digestate is used as a recycled product/material; does not include controlled combustion (incineration) or land application. Should distinguish between mineral waste and other waste. Requires a consolidation and strengthening of waste statistics. Municipal waste recycling could be used as proxy and to reflect efforts by citizens and households. To be read together with information on other recovery types and on waste going to final disposal.
	○ Recycling or recovery rates for selected waste or material types (e.g bio-waste, WEEE, plastics; packaging, construction and demolition waste)	Comp	H	M	OECD MFRP ; EU MF	Complements the national recycling rate. Can be related to indicators on targets and distance to targets below to monitor policy outcomes. Should distinguish between recycling and other recovery operations.
	○ Incineration with energy recovery	Comp	M	H		Could complement the national recycling rate. Not directly linked to circularity; relevance depends on country context and policy objectives.
	○ Capacity of waste recovery infrastructure, by type (recycling, incineration with energy recovery, other recovery)	Comp	M	M		Interpretation: Capacity does not reveal whether waste is effectively recycled. To be read with information on actual recovery rates and on related infrastructure investments. Could be qualified as a contextual indicator. To be read with information on the population with access to (i) waste management services (distinguishing between basic waste collection and separate collection services), and (ii) circularity options (i.e. recycling, composting, repair, etc.).
2.5 Materials leaving the economic cycle	**Waste going to final disposal** (landfill or incineration w/o energy recovery): total; by type of materials	**Core**	H	H/L	OECD MFRP; WP3 Core	Reflects the amounts of materials leaving the economic cycle. Accounts for domestic waste going to final disposal in the country and abroad. Examples of material types include plastics, organic materials. Requires an appropriate breakdown in waste statistics or accounts.
3. Interactions with trade *(see also "opportunities" below)*						
3.1 Trade in materials	○ Material exports, material imports (incl. in RMe) ○ Physical trade balance (incl. in RMe)	Comp	M	H	OECD MFRP	Trade in materials can be a driver for CE policies and CE policies can influence trade. Could be qualified as contextual indicators.
	○ Material intensity of trade flows (trade value indicator)	Comp	M	H	OECD MFRP	Material intensity= net weight/value of goods traded; Trade value indicator = value/net weight of goods traded; (aggregated indicator or per product type or material).

Framework themes and indicator topics	Proposed indicators (a)	Type (b)	Rel. (c)	Meas. (d)	Related indic. sets (e)	Comments
3.2 Trade in CE related materials and products	o Trade in waste, secondary materials, secondary raw materials, second-hand goods, end of life products (proportion in imports, in exports)	Comp	M	M	OECD MFRP	Equally relevant for "opportunities".
Interactions with the environment (environmental effectiveness) *(to be supplemented with other environmental indicators as appropriate)*						
1. Natural resource implications *(physical evolution of natural assets)*						
1.1 Changes in natural resource stocks	**Natural resource index:** non-renewable assets (energy and mineral resources) / **Depletion ratios:** by type of material or asset (extraction over existing reserves)	Core	M	M/L	OECD MFRP, GGI	Most relevant indicator and calculation method to be identified. Level of application (tbd): national, global. Data available for mineral and energy sub-soil resources (accounts) for selected "resource rich" countries by type of stock. Could be used as a proxy. See: OECD Statistical Platform (Code: NAT_RES) and (Schreyer and Obst, 2015[34]).
	o Domestic extraction from natural stocks (renewable & non-renewable) (trends; mix)	Comp	M	H	OECD MFRP	To be derived from economy-wide material flow accounts. To be expanded with information on unused extraction (see below).
	o Changes in natural stocks (global) of mineral resources	Ctx	M	M		Provides global context.
	Intensity of use of renewable freshwater resources: water stress (abstraction over available renewable stocks)	Core	H	M	OECD CEI, GGI; SDG 6.4.2; WP3 Core	Reflects the (potential) pressure on renewable freshwater resources from abstraction during material extraction, processing and use (total freshwater abstraction). To be derived from water statistics and accounts. Should distinguish between freshwater abstraction during the production of goods and services (material extraction, processing, manufacturing) and freshwater abstraction during the consumption (use) of materials.
	o Intensity of use of forest resources (proportion of removals over growth)	Comp	H	M	OECD CEI	To be derived from forest resource accounts or from forest inventories.
1.2 Other natural resource impacts	o Water abstracted for material extraction and processing	Comp	M	M		To be read with (i) water stress reflecting total freshwater abstraction from material extraction, processing and use, and (ii) water discharges and safe treatment. Sector scope to be confirmed and aligned with other similar indicators (GHG, air, water pollution).
	o Water footprint of selected products or sectors	Comp	M	M		
	o Natural resource residuals: Unused extraction (by material group)	Comp	M	L		Refers to unused domestic extraction. Complements domestic extraction used. Could be related to information on potential impacts on habitats and ecosystems.
2. Environmental quality implications *(effects of material extraction, processing, use, and end-of-life management on environmental conditions and human health)*						
2.1 Impacts on climate	**GHG emissions from production activities** (trends, intensities) – Total GHG emissions	Core	H	M H	WP3 Core, EU MF	To be derived from air emission accounts (SEEA). Refers to emissions from the production of goods and services. Total emissions from GHG inventories could be used as a proxy.
	o Proportion of emissions from waste management or waste sector	Comp	M	M	WP3	Complements the core indicator by showing the contribution of waste management to GHG emissions. Could further be supplemented with "proportion of emissions from resource intensive sector" and "proportion of emissions and removals from land use, land use change and forestry".

Framework themes and indicator topics	Proposed indicators (a)	Type (b)	Rel. (c)	Meas. (d)	Related indic. sets (e)	Comments
	○ Carbon footprint (CO_2)	Comp	H	M	WP3 Core	Complements the indicators on GHG emissions. To be read together with the material footprint indicator. Sector scope to be confirmed (all or focus on the production of good and services as for GHG emissions above).
	○ Carbon footprint of priority materials or products, of selected sectors	Comp	M	L	OECD MFRP	Complements the C footprint indicator. The materials, products, sectors to be covered need to be selected. To build on material systems analysis and life-cycle assessments.
2.2 Impacts on air quality	○ Air pollutant emissions from production activities (trends, intensities)	Comp	M	M		To be derived from air emission accounts (SEEA). Refers to emissions from the production of goods and services. The pollutants to be covered need to be selected (e.g. PM2.5).
2.3 Impacts on water and soil quality	**Pollutant discharges from production activities to water bodies & proportion safely treated** – Total discharges to water bodies & % safely treated	Core	H	M	OECD CEI; WP3 Core: safe treat.	Discharges from material extraction and processing and their safe treatment. The pollutants to be covered need to be identified (e.g. heavy metals, nutrients). Sector scope to be confirmed and aligned with other similar indicators (GHG, air, water abstraction). Link to SDG 6.3.1. Total discharges to water bodies & % safely treated could be used as proxy.
	○ Proportion of waste improperly managed (proxy for waste leakage) ○ Number of uncontrolled open landfills	Comp	M	M		Important indicators for countries confronted with basic waste management issues. Could otherwise be qualified as contextual indicators.
	Placeholder: Soil contamination	Comp	M			Soil contamination due to material extraction & processing and end-of-life management.
2.4 Impacts on biodiversity	Placeholders: Impacts from material extraction, processing, use and end-of-life management on land, habitats and species	Comp	H	M		Possible indicators: land cover change with focus on the spatial occupation of the built environment; change in forest cover; land footprint. Indicator reflecting the impacts of marine plastics would also be relevant. Developing and measuring such indicators would require a consensus on the methodologies to use (e.g. life cycle based assessments).
2.5 Impacts on human health	**Placeholder**	Core	H			Most relevant impacts and core indicator to be identified. To be read with information on the baseline socio-economic distribution of environmental goods and bads, when available.
	Population exposure to air pollution; related premature deaths and welfare costs	Comp	M	M		To be derived from EO sources. See the WHO Global Burden of Disease project. See the OECD datasets on environmental health and risks.
	Placeholder: Water-related health impacts	Comp	M			See WHO Global Burden of Disease project. Most relevant indicator to be identified.
	Placeholder: population groups living in the vicinity of waste management sites and production sites	Comp	M			Most relevant indicator and calculation method to be identified. Links to well-being and environmental justice.
Responses and actions (policies, measures, framework conditions)						*(most indicators proposed here require further work and research)*
1. Support circular use of materials, promote recycling markets and optimise design						
1.1 Measures supporting circular business models and encouraging reuse,	**Taxes & government support for circular business models** – VAT relief and tax credits for refurbished/repaired items – Tax benefits for businesses for the purchase/use of repaired, refurbished, remanufactured items	Core	H	M	OECD, Eurostat, WP3 Core	Most relevant core indicator and calculation method to be identified. Requires a definition of circular business models in the context of tax systems. CE relevant subsidies and other government support (including tax reliefs and exemptions) to be identified. Measurement boundaries to be specified.

Framework themes and indicator topics	Proposed indicators (a)	Type (b)	Rel. (c)	Meas. (d)	Related indic. sets (e)	Comments
repair, remanufacturing *(incl. industrial ecology/ symbiosis & sharing models)*	– Trade tariffs: Import/export taxes for re-used & refurbished equipment compared to taxes on new equipment – Subsidies and other transfers supporting a CE					Could be derived from accounts on 'Environmental subsidies and similar transfers' building on the SEEA (e.g. Eurostat), from inventories of government support, from databases on policy instruments (e.g. OECD PINE database) and from environmentally related tax revenue accounts building on the SEEA and other tax revenue accounts.
	o Circular Public Procurement (CPP) or Green Public procurement (GPP): total; by type of good (proportion in total public procurement)	Comp	H	L	EU MF, WP3 Core	CPP could be a core indicator. GPP to be considered as a proxy. Links to SDG 12.7.1: Degree of sustainable public procurement policies and action plan implementation. PP accounts for a large share of consumption and can drive the circular economy transition and innovation.
	o Investments in infrastructure supporting circular business models, beyond waste management (e.g. repair facilities).	Comp	H	L		Most relevant indicator, data sources and calculation methods to be identified. To be read with information on % of population with access to circularity options (e.g. repair services)
	o Population with access to circularity options (e.g. repair services) (proportion in total population)	Ctx	H	L		To be complemented with information on the proportion of population with access to waste management services.
1.2 Measures encouraging eco-design	Design for extending lifespans (i.e. durability, repairability, upgradeability): o Requirements for minimum lifespan, warranties, software upgrades o Requirements for accessibility to spare parts	Comp	H	M		Most relevant indicator and calculation methods to be identified. It remains to be seen whether this topic can be measured in the form of an indicator or whether it should be qualified as "other relevant information to be considered".
	Design for recycling, dismantling & material circularity: o Bans/Guidelines on hazardous substances o Taxes on difficult-to-recycle items o Availability of guidance documents on design for recycling	Comp	H	M		Most relevant indicator and calculation methods to be identified. It remains to be seen whether this topic can be measured in the form of an indicator or whether it should be qualified as "other relevant information to be considered".
1.3 Measures encouraging efficient use of materials and economically efficient waste recovery	o Reform of subsidies encouraging unsustainable use or extraction of materials, e.g., taxes on virgin materials	Comp	H	M		Could be expanded to cover economic instruments encouraging linearity.
	Extended Producer Responsibility (EPR) schemes: o Availability of EPR schemes in different product sectors: distance between reported performance and set target	Comp	M	M		Product sectors could include: automobiles, batteries, tyres, packaging, pharmaceuticals, textiles, etc. Distance could be zero if legally binding performance target is not available. Could be used as a core indicator by countries.
	Deposit-refund systems (DRS) & Pay-as-you-throw (PAYT) schemes: o Availability of DRS in different product sectors (scope of beverage containers, for reuse & recycling) o Availability of PAYT schemes	Comp	M	H/M		Best way to calculate and present these indicators to be identified. To be complemented with stringency indicators e.g. the disposal cost difference between different waste types. Could be qualified as "other relevant information to be considered".

Framework themes and indicator topics	Proposed indicators (a)	Type (b)	Rel. (c)	Meas. (d)	Related indic. sets (e)	Comments
2. Improve the efficiency of waste management and close leakage pathways						
2.1 Measures to improve waste management	**Investments in waste management infrastructure, waste collection and sorting:** government, businesses	Core	H	M	EU MF; WP3 Core	To be derived from environmental expenditure accounts (SEEA). If data availability permits, could be expanded with information on investments in (i) repair, reuse & waste prevention infrastructure; (ii) energy recovery of waste; (iii) sound disposal of waste
	o Population with access to waste management services: basic waste collection; separate collection (proportion in total population)	Ctx	M	H		Important information for countries confronted with basic waste management issues. To be complemented with information on the proportion of population with access to circularity options (i.e. recycling, composting, repair services, etc.)
2.2. Measures to encourage waste reduction	o Bans, taxes on frequently littered items or single-use items (e.g. plastics)	Comp	H	H		Best way to calculate these indicators to be identified.
	o Tax rate per tonne landfilled or incinerated	Comp	H	H		Could be derived from the OECD PINE database. Important indicator for countries with waste management challenges.
	o Landfill bans	Comp	H	H		Important indicator for countries with waste management challenges.
3. Boost innovation and orient technological change						
3.1 Measures supporting R&D	**Government and business R&D expenditure on CE technologies** (recycling, secondary raw materials, …): budget allocations	Core	H	M/L		Allocating data on R&D budgets to circular projects/topics is not easy. The measurement boundaries need to be specified.
3.2 Technology development and international diffusion	o Patented inventions for (1) recycling and secondary raw materials; and (2) reuse and repair models as:	Comp	M	M/L	OECD ; EU MF ; WP3 Core	Innovative technologies related to the CE can boost countries' global competitiveness. Patents however only give only a limited view on what is being invented. Little data are available on patents for repair and reuse models. Indicators equally relevant for "opportunities".
	– % of total technologies, by inventor's residence – % of foreign inventors, by patent office	Comp	M	M/L		
4. Target setting and planning						
4.1 Targets & distance to targets	Placeholder: Distance to targets	Comp				Most relevant indicators to be identified. Indicators on targets take on their full meaning when linked to associated material life cycle indicators ("waste generation" & "recycling" indicators) and when revealing how distance to targets changes over time; they are particularly relevant when used in a national context. Interpretation needs to consider that targets vary across countries and depend on national circumstances and levels of ambition. Could be core indicators for countries. N.B. Monitoring recycled content targets and reuse targets is challenging. To be applied to selected products (plastics, food, packaging, …).
	– Resource productivity targets	Comp	H	H	WP3 Core	
	– Recycled content targets, by type of product	Comp	H	M/L		
	– Recycling targets, by type of waste	Comp	H	H		
	– Reuse targets, by type of product	Comp	H	L		
	– Waste reduction/prevention targets by waste type	Comp	H	H		
	– Landfill targets, distance to targets by waste type	Comp	M	H		Important indicator for countries with waste management challenges.
4.2 CE strategies & plans	Placeholder	Comp	M			Most relevant indicator and calculation method to be identified. It remains to be seen whether this topic can be measured in the form of an indicator or whether it should be qualified as "other relevant information to be considered". Plans and strategies to be considered include those fostering a CE, industrial upgrading, competitiveness and productivity, innovation.

Framework themes and indicator topics	Proposed indicators (a)	Type (b)	Rel. (c)	Meas. (d)	Related indic. sets (e)	Comments
5. Strengthen financial flows						
5.1 Domestic financial flows	**Business investment in CE activities**	Core	H	M	EU MF. WP3 Core	To be derived from environmental expenditure accounts and accounts on environmental goods and services (SEEA), national accounts and structural business statistics. Could be linked to indicators on jobs and value added in the CE sector (cf EU MF) and to indicators on subsidies and other transfers supporting CE sectors to open up additional analyses. Data availability is best for investment in reuse and recycling activities and in EU countries. Other activities such as renting and leasing could be added in future; current statistics are not granular enough to provide a means of distinguishing activities that clearly contribute to a circular economy transition from those that do not.
	o Revenue from CE related taxes	Comp	H	H/M		Could be derived from the OECD PINE database or from environmentally related tax revenue accounts building on the SEEA. Requires a consensus on the measurement boundaries.
	o Government budgets allocated to CE objectives	Comp	H	M		Country-specific indicator. Could be derived from green budgeting initiatives in countries.
5.2 International financial flows	o CE related Official Development Assistance (ODA)	Comp	M	L		Data on financial flows related to waste management exist. CE related flows are more difficult to identify. The measurement boundaries need to be specified.
	o CE related Foreign Direct Investment (FDI)	Comp	M	L		
6. Inform, educate and train						
6.1 Information instruments	Placeholders o Eco-labelling; product labelling & certificates o Requirement to provide repair guidelines o Requirement to provide: – information on expected lifespan; dismantling guidelines & material content lists for recyclers	Comp	M	M/L		Most relevant indicators and calculation methods to be defined; data sources to be identified. It remains to be seen whether this topic can be measured in the form of an indicator or whether it should be qualified as "other relevant information to be considered".
6.2 Education and training	**Placeholder: Integration of CE issues in school curricula and professional training**	Core	H			Most relevant indicators and calculation methods to be defined; data sources to be identified.
Socio-economic opportunities for a just transition *(economic efficiency and social equity)*						
1. Market developments and new business models						
1.1 CE entrepreneurship, goods & services (incl. uptake of new circular business models, industrial ecology/symbiosis initiatives)	**Gross value added of CE sectors** (% contribution to GDP and change over time)	Core	H	H/L	EU MF; WP3 Core	Reflects the contribution of a circular economy to the creation of growth. To be derived from national accounts or Environmental goods and services sector (SEEA). Trend in indicator value is more important than absolute values. Data availability is best for CE sectors delineated as waste and recycling. Should be expanded to include repair services and second-hand markets as data availability progresses. Could be complemented with information on power production from renewable sources (cf SDG 7.b.1/12.a.1 and WP3 Core)
	o CE start-ups and trademarks o CE certification of companies	Comp	M	L		Indicators to be defined. Data sources to be identified.

Framework themes and indicator topics	Proposed indicators (a)	Type (b)	Rel. (c)	Meas. (d)	Related indic. sets (e)	Comments
1.2 Employment markets and jobs	**Jobs in CE sectors** (proportion in total employment and change over time)	Core	H	H/L	EU MF, WP3 Core	Reflects the contribution of a circular economy to the creation of jobs. Trend in indicator value is more important than absolute values. Requires a consensus on the measurement boundaries (sectors and job types to be covered). To be derived from accounts on the environmental goods and services sector (EGSS) available in EU countries. CE sectors delineated as waste and recycling. To be expanded as data availability progresses to include other CE activities, including repair services, second-hand markets and sharing economy. (cf also the EU taxonomy of sustainable activities).
	Jobs in sharing economy, reuse and repair activities (number and change over time)	Comp	H	L		Complements the core indicator by providing additional detail on the sharing economy, repair and reuse activities. Trend in indicator value is more important than absolute values. Data on repair activities may be more available than data on jobs in the sharing economy or in reuse services. Alternative data sources are needed.
1.3 Recycling markets	Markets for recycled materials	Comp	H	L		Indicator to be defined. To focus on materials of particular importance from an environmental and economic point of view (e.g. construction, plastics, metals)
2. Trade developments						
2.1 Trade in CE related goods and services	o Trade in recovered (secondary) materials (volume, proportion in imports & exports)	Comp	M	M/L		Trade in recovered, recycled and recyclable materials reflects the importance of the domestic market and global participation in a circular economy. Requires a common definition of "recyclable" materials. "Recyclability" is challenging to define. Technical and economic factors play a role. To be read with "interactions with trade" under "material life cycle" above. To be expanded to a broader set of CE-related goods and services as data availability progresses.
	o Trade in recycled (secondary raw) materials (volume, proportion in imports & exports)	Comp	M	M/L	OECD MFRP	
	o Trade in recyclable raw materials (proportion in imports & exports)	Comp	M	L	EU MF	
2.2 Supply security	Domestic material autonomy: aggregate, by material group a. proportion of domestic extraction in DMI or DMC b. proportion of domestic extraction in RMI or RMC	Comp	H	H	OECD MFRP, EU MF, WP3 Core	Double-headed indicator. To be read with "interactions with trade" under "material life cycle". Material autonomy can in some countries be an important driver for moving towards a CE. A CE can create opportunities for reducing reliance on external markets and increasing the resilience to imports of critical raw materials which is especially of concern for resource importing countries.[2] Could otherwise be qualified as a contextual indicator.
	o Supply security of "strategic" raw materials: by material or material group	Comp	H	M	OECD MFRP, EU MF	A CE helps address the supply risks for raw materials, in particular "strategic" materials (raw and processed or semi-processed). Materials to be considered may vary across countries and regions. Could be a core indicator if common strategic raw materials are identified. What to classify as "strategic" materials needs to be specified. Needs to consider economic & environmental factors. Different methodologies exist to assess material criticality (e.g. (Coulomb et al., 2015[35]; Graedel et al., 2012[36])). See also (European Commission, 2024[37])
	o Food security o Energy security	Comp	H	M		A CE helps also satisfy human consumption needs and address supply risks. Both food and energy could be considered as strategic materials (see above).

Framework themes and indicator topics	Proposed indicators (a)	Type (b)	Rel. (c)	Meas. (d)	Related indic. sets (e)	Comments
3. Skills, awareness and behaviour						
3.1 Skills	Placeholders o CE literacy ; CE skills	Comp	H			Most relevant indicators to be identified. Could among others cover: innovation competencies to support the transition to a CE (in secondary schools, in higher education); education in upskilling and reskilling.
3.2 Awareness	o Public opinion on CE issues and actions	Comp	M	L		
3.3 Behaviour	**Placeholder: Change in household, consumer, firm behaviour**	Core	H			Indicators on behaviour can help identify the right policy measures to achieve a successful transition.
4. Inclusiveness of the transition						
	Placeholder: Distributional aspects & socio-economic inequality of CE policies	Core	M			Requires further work and research. Is closely related to "environmental justice"; Would reflect how different territories and population groups (young people, women, vulnerable communities, etc.) are affected or benefit from CE policies and actions or endure impacts from inaction. To be broken down by population groups and by location when possible. Could also reflect whether a disproportionate share of communities endure impacts as a result of materials use (i.e. population living close to landfills/incinerators, population living close to production facilities. To be complemented with more general inequality indicators (see below). To be read with information on the baseline socio-economic distribution of environmental goods and bads when available.
Socio-economic and environmental context						
1. Factors that drive demand for materials						
1.1 Socio-demographic factors	o Population growth and structure o Household size	Ctx	M	H		
1.2 Economic factors	o GDP growth and structure (trends, value added by sector)	Ctx	M	H		
	o Income levels: GDP per capita	Ctx	M	H		Could be broken down by population groups and by location when possible. Could be supplemented with debt-to-income ratio, poverty index, energy poverty, employment rates, etc.
	o Income inequality (Gini index); wealth inequality	Ctx	M	H/M		
	o Human development index (HDI)	Ctx	M	H		
	o Final consumption expenditure: government, household	Ctx	M	H		
1.3 Sectoral drivers	o Construction e.g., floor space per capita, value added of construction sector	Ctx	H	M/L		
	o Other					

Framework themes and indicator topics	Proposed indicators (a)	Type (b)	Rel. (c)	Meas. (d)	Related indic. sets (e)	Comments
2. Factors that influence the environmental implications of material use						
2.1 Environmental drivers	o Energy supply and consumption: trends and intensities	Ctx	H	H		Could be considered core or complementary indicators in countries whose CE policies address the efficiency and circularity of energy and water.
	o Water use efficiency in production activities and in final consumption	Ctx	H	M		
	o Protected areas	Ctx	M	H/M		
	o Other					

1. Circular input use rate (Japan): Share of recycled materials (secondary raw materials) in material inputs, for selected materials or material groups, i.e. recycled amounts/(DMI+recycled amounts).
2. The OECD Global Materials Resources Outlook to 2060 provides information on materials criticality (OECD, 2019[2]).

Note

[1] See the Communication from the Commission to the European Parliament, the Council, the European Economic and Social Committee and the Committee of the Regions on a revised monitoring framework for the circular economy (European Commission, 2023[16]). See also Eurostat's general overview of the EU CE Monitoring Framework (Eurostat, 2024[55]).

Annex B. Existing measurement frameworks and indicators

This Annex presents a selection of monitoring frameworks to assess the progress towards a circular economy in countries and the European Union. It is not a comprehensive overview of available frameworks, but rather aims to illustrate different approaches that informed the conceptual monitoring framework outlined in this report and to identify synergies and commonalities among existing indicator sets in terms of structure and indicators chosen.

Box B.1. Summary of main differences and commonalities in reviewed monitoring frameworks

In the past ten years, efforts directed at developing measurement frameworks and indicators for measuring progress towards a circular economy have expanded. The indicator sets in use or being developed are often country specific and developed in consultation with stakeholders and through dialogues between policy makers and statisticians. Therefore, their structure and the topics covered vary across countries.

This Annex provides a detailed review of select monitoring frameworks, which vary in genesis, size, scope and conceptual underpinning.

- The *genesis* and context in which a monitoring framework was developed differs. Whilst some were developed as extension of environmental metrics (e.g. Colombia), others were linked to a specific CE policy strategy (e.g. France). Some were developed within the governmental ministries, whilst others were the output of research consortia (e.g. Flanders and The Netherlands).
- The scope and the number of indicators varies depending on the purpose for which the indicators are to be used (between 11 and 151 indicators in the reviewed indicator sets). All monitoring frameworks group indicators into sub-themes to create further structure. In the frameworks with larger number of indicators, the themes may also serve to give some prioritisation. Most indicator frameworks are associated with regular reporting (e.g. the Netherlands, Japan).
- Some frameworks represent material flow indicators as relative values, in form of resource efficiency or per-capita indicators (e.g. China, France, EU), other frameworks present absolute values (the Netherlands, Flanders). Some frameworks offer both types of values together (Japan, Colombia). The latter approach has the advantage of conveying a more balanced message: relative indicators provide comparability between countries and demonstrate relative progress, whereas absolute indicators highlight the size of material flows.
- There are remarkable differences in the materials considered: some include water and energy besides the more typical material flows. In the case of China energy and water are even highlighted. Broad material flow indicators are missing from the Colombian framework, while here forestry products are highlighted. Also, the choice whether and how to include the *Domestic Material Consumption* indicator differs.
- An important consideration is the resilience with respect to future modifications of the indicator sets, to accommodate changes in how the CE may be conceived, in targets and in data availability. For instance, in recent years the role of a CE transition in reaching enhanced emission reductions has been emphasised and including greenhouse gas emission indicators into CE monitoring frameworks may become more central. A robust conceptual framework that is more amenable to accommodate modifications and additions enables more a dynamic monitoring process (e.g. the French framework was revised and updated).

The way the monitoring frameworks and indicators are disseminated is also important. Most frameworks and indicators are available in the form of progress reports (e.g. Japan, the Netherlands, Colombia, France), other frameworks publish data in interactive online tools (European Union, Flanders).

Japan

In Japan, policies related to implementing a CE are centred around the concept of a "Sound Material-Cycle Society", first enacted by the Basic Act for Establishing a Sound-Material Cycle Society in 2000. In 2003 the Japanese government adopted its Fundamental Plan for Establishing a Sound Material-Cycle Society, which is reviewed and revised every five years by the Ministry of Environment Japan (MOEJ). The Fundamental Plan and its targets were last revised in 2018 (MOEJ, 2018[38]; Bangert, 2020[39]).

The development of the Plan was motivated by Japan's high rate of waste generation, limited availability of land space for waste disposal, increasing public demand for recycling, supply security concerns of raw materials and Japan's heavy import reliance. The plan is aligned with Japan's waste and recycling policies, and aims to provide comprehensive measures for materials management, including upstream consumption and downstream waste management and recycling measures (Geng et al., 2012[40]).

The Plan for Establishing a Sound Material-Cycle Society is supported with quantitative time-bound targets and performance indicators. Stakeholders are asked to contribute to their achievement. The targets and the associated indicators are used to monitor progress, assess each stakeholder's efforts and encourage further action. The Plan includes targets on resource productivity, cyclical use rate (defined at the level of resources and of waste), and on landfilled waste (MOEJ, 2018[41]). The targets are monitored by a framework consisting of a set of 151 indicators, with four headline indicators. The FY2025 targets set in the 4th Plan for the four headline indicators are:

- *Resource Productivity* [GDP/Input of natural resources]: 490,000 JPY / ton (approximately double from FY2000)
- *Cyclical use rate* [amount of cyclical use/(amount of cyclical use + input of natural resources)]: 18% (approximately 80% increase from FY2000)
- *Cyclical use rate (waste base)* [amount of cyclical use / generation of waste]: 47% (approximately 30% increase from FY2000)
- *Final disposal* [amount of waste destined for landfills]: 13 million tonnes: 77% decrease from FY2000)

Supplementary indicators refer to different elements of the transition process and societal efforts towards realising a CE and track various elements of material input (material consumption), circularity (recycling rates), material output (waste generation), efforts on regional level, household behaviour, consumer awareness (e.g. through survey results), business operations (e.g. market size of circular business models) and actions in the public sector (e.g. public procurement) (MOEJ, 2018[41]; EASAC, 2016[42]) (Table B.1). Indicator scores are updated yearly and available starting from 2000. The indicators are published in the Annual report on the Environment, the Sound Material-Cycle Society and Biodiversity in Japan, and progress reports are being emitted regularly (MOEJ, 2010[43]; MOEJ, 2013[44]; MOEJ, 2018[38]).

Table B.1. Material flow and resource productivity indicators in Japan

Overview indicators and associated targets for FY 2025	
Indicators	Targets for FY 2025
1. Resource Productivity	490 000JPY/tonne, i.e. approx. a doubling of FY 2000
2. Cyclical Use Rate (resource based)	18%, i.e. ~ 80% increase from FY 2000
3. Cyclical Use Rate (waste based)	47%, i.e. ~ 30% increase from FY 2000
4. Final Disposal Amount of waste	13 million tonnes, i.e. a 77% cut from FY 2000
II. Thematic material flow indicators (some associated with targets)	
1. Resource productivity by industry	6. Ratio of domestically-produced biomass resources to total natural resource inputs
2. Generation of household food waste	7. Per-capita waste generation per day
3. Generation of commercial food waste	8. Per-capita household waste generation per day
4. Emission of greenhouse gas from the waste sector	9. Business waste generation
5. Reduction of GHG emissions from other sectors through using waste as raw materials and fuel for power generation	10. Amount of illegal dumping
	11. Amount of waste treated improperly
III. Thematic management indicators (some associated with targets)	
1. Market size of sound material-cycle society business	12. Diffusion rate of electronic manifests
2. Average power generation efficiency of waste incineration facilities constructed/improved during the period	13. Remaining sustainable years of final disposal sites for municipal waste
3. Area of forests with specific forest management plans	14. Remaining sustainable years of final disposal sites for industrial waste
4. Number of local governments working on Regional circular and ecological sphere	15. Share of local governments having a disaster waste management plan
5. Size of reuse market	16. Number of nations with which a memorandum of understanding/agreement on environmental cooperation (including for resource recycling) is signed
6. Size of sharing economy market	17. Number of recycling businesses promoting overseas expansion
7. Guidelines for product assessment by industries (design for environment)	18. Share of research projects on sound material cycles
8. Implementation rate of recycling of cyclical food resources	19. Waste reduction and awareness for cyclical use and green purchase
9. Establishment rate of life extension plans for individual facilities (individual facility plan)	20. Implementation rate of specific 3R actions
10. Number of illegal dumping cases	
11. Number of improper waste treatment cases	

Source: Country contribution to the annual Round Table on Environmental Information (WPEI) and http://www.env.go.jp/en/wpaper/

The focus of the Fundamental Plan appears to be predominantly on domestic environmental and economic issues related to materials. With the circular use rate as one of the headline targets, the "circular economy" is also partially framed as a goal in itself, as opposed to a means to obtaining other goals. The transition process and the broader effects on the environment, economy and society are less visible within the framework and only covered to some extent in the supplementary indicators. For instance, emissions are only covered to the extent that these occur from waste management. Currently, transboundary issues related to material consumption and impacts are not considered in the framework, but the development of such indicators has been announced (MOEJ, 2018[41]). The lead indicator on resource productivity is based on Direct Material Inputs, not subtracting exports. However, data on Domestic Material Consumption and absolute material flows are available in other parts of the monitoring framework and there are discussions to compute the material footprint indicator, once a methodology has been established (MOEJ, 2018[41]).

Table B.2. Summary of Japan's indicator framework

Description	A set of four headline indicators and 151 supplementary indicators developed in the wake of a policy plan focusing on issues of waste disposal and access to raw materials.
Indicator coverage	Material consumption, recycling, waste production. Lead indicators are GDP/DMI, cyclical material use rate and waste sent to landfill, all connected to targets. The other indicators cover more aspects e.g. transition process, societal efforts, economic parameters, more detailed waste data.
Actual or intended use of indicators	Indicators are updated yearly and connect to a plan reviewed every five years. Targets have been formulated for the four lead indicators. Progress reports are regularly emitted.
Information gaps	The structure of the framework rather frames material circularity and the "circular economy" as a goal itself that is desirable to be reached; indicators pertaining to the broader transition are more difficult to retrieve. Indirect material use is currently not covered. Emissions are only considered in relation to waste management.

China

Since 2008 the Circular Economy Promotion Law drives the transition towards a CE in China. The associated monitoring comprises two separate indicator sets: one that helps to monitor progress on national and regional levels, and one that applies to industrial parks. The indicator sets provide guidance to CE development planning (Geng et al., 2012[40]).

The indicator set for *national and regional analysis* contains 22 indicators, categorised into four main themes. The theme "resource output rate" tracks outputs of main mineral resources and of energy. The theme "resource consumption rate" focuses on energy and water consumption divided by three denominators: Gross Domestic Product, added value and the amount of produced materials. The theme "resource utilisation" focuses on recycling of different material streams including metals, paper, plastics and wastewater and the theme "waste disposal and pollutant emissions", includes indicators on waste sent to landfill, wastewater discharges and emissions air (Geng et al., 2012[40]).

The indicator set for *industrial parks* contains 12 indicators, categorised into the same four main themes. The indicator set is similar, but provides additional information on water and energy consumption per unit of key product.

While the two indicator sets cover a variety of aspects of a CE, the monitoring framework has some limitations, notably (Geng et al., 2012[40]):

- Consumption indicators are only included as efficiency indicators (divided by GDP or per unit of output produced). This reflects progress to a more resource efficient economy, but it hides overall material consumption.
- Waste indicators only indicate the amount of waste destined for disposal, but not the overall amount of waste generated. Similarly, recycling rates are only available for specific waste streams, but no overall recycling rate.
- The indicator set focuses largely on environmental impacts but is lacking indicators on social implications. It also lacks indicators on business activities, circular business models and the higher Rs more generally.
- There is no consideration of value chains outside the country territory and impacts embedded in imports or exports.
- Indicators on environmental implications refer to wastewater discharges emissions of SO2 and chemical oxygen demand. Greenhouse gas emissions are not included but appear to be retrievable beyond this indicator set at the Department for Climate Change Response. Several other ecological indicators appear to be available at the Ministry of Environmental Protection with a city focus, which could also complement this framework.
- No information is available on targets associated with the indicators, nor on follow-up progress assessments or revisions of the indicator set.

Table B.3. Summary of China's indicator framework

Description	A set of 22 indicators developed to provide guidance to CE development planning in the wake of the Circular Economy Promotion Law
Indicator coverage	Resource productivity, resource consumption, utilisation rate and waste generation. Focus on consumption of energy, water and materials, business activities, recycling, landfilling and pollutant emissions.
Actual or intended use of the indicators	No information available.
Information gaps	Absolute material consumption levels, primary waste production, greenhouse gas emissions, indirect material use, socio-economic aspects focus on industrial value

France

The French framework for monitoring the circular economy was first published in 2017, comprising 11 indicators (Magnier, 2017[45]). It was updated and revised in 2021 (Scribe et al., 2021[46]). It was inspired by the emerging publications on the CE of the European Commission and is designed to benchmark France's performance against other European countries. Many indicators are available on EU28 level.

France uses a measurement framework and indicators that cover the following dimensions of a CE transition: the supply side (sustainable extraction and manufacturing, eco-design, industrial ecology, employment), the demand side (consumer behaviour, sharing economy initiatives), product management aspects (second-hand, repair, reuse) and waste management aspects (waste prevention, recycling). Eleven indicators within seven pillars are used to report on the circularity of the French economy (Table B.4).

Table B.4. Indicators of the French monitoring framework

Pillar	Indicator
Extraction / manufacturing and sustainable supply chain	Domestic material consumption per capita
	Resource productivity
	Material footprint *(new since 2021)*
Eco-design (products and processes)	European ecolabel
Industrial symbiosis	Number of industrial symbiosis initiatives
Functional economy	Number of companies and local authorities that have benefited from government support mechanisms on the functional economy
Responsible consumption	Food waste
Extension of product lifespan	Household spending on product maintenance and repair (excluding vehicle maintenance)
Recycling (material and organic)	Landfill tonnage trend
	Use of secondary raw materials in production processes
	Jobs in the repair of goods and recycling of materials

Source: (Scribe et al., 2021[46])

The indicator scoreboard marks individual indicators in colours, depending on the extent to which the indicator score evolves in the desirable direction. Two of the indicators are connected to national CE targets (i.e. resource productivity and waste sent to landfill) (Scribe et al., 2021[46]).

Overall, the indicator set has a strong focus on the material consumption aspect. Indicators on environmental implications are not considered. With regards to recycling, the use of secondary raw materials is monitored, but not the recycling rate in itself. The indicator list includes several indicators on the higher Rs, such as jobs in repair and household spending on repair and maintenance services. Also eco-design aspects are considered. Whilst the monitoring framework covers a diverse set of indicators, the diversity of individual indicators makes it challenging to compare progress and trends of individual indicators. Also, several data limitations are acknowledged for some of the chosen indicators, which have been partially improved in the 2021 revision (Scribe et al., 2021[46]).

Table B.5. Summary of France's indicator framework

Description	A dashboard of 11 indicators published by the national statistics service incited by French and European policy initiatives
Indicator coverage	Four main indicator themes: supply, consumption, waste and employment. Different aspects of the transition are highlighted, ranging from material consumption and waste to transition actions at the level of companies and consumers.
Actual or intended use of the indicators	Indicator scores and the indicator set have been updated in 2021. The indicators on Resource productivity and on waste sent to landfill directly connect to French CE targets.
Information gaps	The collection reflects the transition in a broad way but is too limited to cover it accordingly. Some aspects are missing e.g. waste production, recycling rates, absolute material consumption. Environmental effects are not considered.

The Netherlands

The Dutch Environmental Assessment Agency and Statistics Netherlands (CBS), together with a consortium of Dutch governmental and knowledge institutions developed a monitoring framework for the Netherlands in 2018 (Potting et al., 2017[5]). The framework was developed to track progress towards Dutch circular economy targets to reduce abiotic resource use by 50% by 2030 and to be completely circular by 2050.

The monitor considers the CE transition in a broad sense by clearly separating the different phases of the transition into input, throughput, output and outcome phases. It also focuses on five priority sectors, which were selected based on economic importance and high environmental burden: 1) biomass and food, 2) plastics, 3) manufacturing industry, 4) construction and 5) consumer goods.

Lead indicators in the Dutch monitoring framework comprise *direct* and *indirect material use* and *consumption*, environmental effects (*land use*, *water extraction*, *residence-based* and *footprint emissions*), socio-economic effects (*economic growth*, *employment aspects of the CE transition*, *added value* and *self-sufficiency*), *waste* and *recycling*. *Renewable energy* is also included. The monitor contains the *size of the economy* and *employment* as so-called autonomous factors as a way to avoid misinterpretations of changes in indicator values that may be due to broader tendencies rather than progress within the CE transition. Next, the monitor displays data on the transition process by listing and counting an elaborated amount of *policy and stakeholder actions* and *realizations* supporting the transition. The monitor additionally contains a Sankey diagram for the Netherlands and furthermore displays indicators disaggregated for five key sectors for which a dedicated transition agreement had been obtained from the government before the development of the monitor. Progress reporting is foreseen biennially, with the first progress report published in 2021 (Hanemaaijer et al., 2021[47]). Shorter focused updates are also published more frequently (Prins and Hanemaaijer, 2022[48]).

The monitor framework is quite comprehensive in terms of scope and selection of indicators. It covers direct and indirect material use, presents absolute indicators besides efficiency indicators and provides GDP and population as context indicators. The framework contains indicators on the broader environmental and socio-economic effects of the transition. It also presents information on the transition process, with the aim to provide a more direct feedback to policy, but given the premature state of development of indicators on this matter the information is qualitative. Interestingly, the Direct Material Consumption indicator is only indirectly displayed in the material productivity indicator. Whilst the framework seems to cover most aspects of the CE transition, gaps remain in terms of data availability for some of the indicators.

Table B.6. Summary of the Dutch indicator framework

Description	Extensive monitoring framework developed to measure progress towards established CE targets and sectoral agreements established by the government.
Indicator coverage	Comprehensive scope, covering all phases of the transition process: input (actors, technology, money), throughput (running actions and projects), output (direct prestation, e.g. material flows) and outcome (indirect effects to the environment (e.g. footprints) and socio-economic).
Actual or intended use of the indicators	Progress assessment conducted biennially, with intermittent focused updates. High-level targets by the national government are not directly reflected in indicators.
Information gaps	Framework is comprehensive in terms of scope, but gaps remain for indicators where data availability is limited.

Colombia

Under Colombia's Sustainability Pact of the National Development Plan 2018-2022, the National Administrative Department of Statistics (DANE) developed a Circular Economy Information System as a strategic pillar of the National Circular Economy Strategy. The system built on environmental statistics that have been created from 2017 (UNECE, 2021[49]).

The monitoring framework comprises 44 indicators, classified into themes along the material cycle: extraction, production, consumption and use, and closing cycles. Particular focus among the indicators is on *mineral reserves* and *extraction*, *forestry products*, *water*, *energy*, *waste*, *greenhouse gas emissions*, *employment*, *government spending*, *added value* and *waste*. A number of indicators are available both as absolute numbers and as intensity values, e.g. indicators on forestry products, water, energy and emissions. Follow-up on the indicator scores has taken place with the publication of, so far, five Circular Economy Reports, focusing on the state and opportunities for Colombia to transition towards more circular production and consumption (DANE, 2022[50]).

In the Colombian indicator set, water and energy are considered as an implicit part of a CE. The dedicated inclusion of forestry products as an individual indictor relates to the importance of this raw material in the Colombian country. A comprehensive material flow analysis is currently not included in the work; but sectoral Sankey diagram were included for energy carriers and their use, carbon emissions, water abstraction and waste generation and fate (DANE, 2022[50]). The key materials that the monitoring framework focuses on are energy carriers, water and forestry products. Data on other materials are largely absent in the reports. As such, the transition process is only limited covered.

Table B.7. Summary of the Colombia's indicator framework

Description	Indicator set of 44 indicators developed under Colombia's Sustainability Pact, maintained by its Department of Statistics in order to inform progress in national CE strategy.
Indicator coverage	Extraction, production, consumption and use, and closing cycles; more specifically mineral reserves and extraction. Strong focus on forestry products, water, energy carriers and waste. Other aspects considered include greenhouse gas emissions, employment, government spending, added value and waste.
Actual or intended use of the indicators	DANE publishes circular economy reports several times per year with new and updated data. No national targets seem to be tied to the monitoring framework and indicator set.
Information gaps	Direct and indirect material flows, transition process.

Region of Flanders (Belgium)

The Flanders Region in Belgium has developed a monitoring tool that focuses on the outputs and outcomes of a CE, with indicators on environmental outcomes (e.g. climate impacts), economic outcomes (e.g. access to materials), societal outcomes (e.g. jobs). The tool includes indicators on product chains, footprint indicators (material and carbon), and indicators that link the CE transition to planetary boundaries, as well as indicators on societal and economic drivers (e.g. mobility, housing, food habits, consumption goods).

Flanders' monitor was published in 2021 as a result of a five-year academic research project dedicated to provide the Flemish government of Belgium with a tool to monitor its transition towards a more circular economy (Circular Flanders, 2022[51]). Since 2017 the Flemish government maintains a long-term policy agenda called Vision 2050 in which the CE transition is considered one of the seven societal transition themes and in which a dedicated public-private cooperation has been installed named Circular Flanders. The process of building the monitor included academic research combined with elaborate stakeholder discussions (Alaerts et al., 2019[52]).

The framework displays a total of about 140 indicators.

- About 25 indicators constitute a top layer of macro indicators that represent the CE transition as a means to reach broader sustainability goals. It includes a separate section for 'circularity' comprising inflows, R-strategies and outflows, and broader environmental and socio-economic effects. The indicators cover among others *Direct* and *Raw Material Input*, *Domestic* and *Raw Material Consumption*, *water consumption*, *waste generation*, *recycling*, *cyclical material use*, an in-house developed *reuse* indicator, *residence-based* and *indirect emissions*, *spatial occupation*, *employment in CE* and *employment in reuse shops*. Indicators about the transition process are almost absent.
- More specific indicators on four systems that fulfil societal needs, including (i) mobility, (ii) buildings and housing, (iii) nutrition, and (iv) consumer goods are available down to the product group level with the aim to provide a more direct feedback to policy. A few of these indicators refer to the transition process, e.g. the amount of car sharing memberships or the number of renovations.

The overall indicator set is available online and will be further maintained and developed in the coming years by the research consortium. In 2019, the Flemish government announced several headline targets for the CE transition, notably on household waste reduction, recycling and a 30% reduction of the material footprint. These targets link to the respective indicators in the monitoring framework.

Table B.8. Summary of the Flemish indicator framework

Description	A set of around 140 indicators at the macro and the meso-level developed on request of the Flemish government, in the wake of the installation of Circular Flanders.
Indicator coverage	Circularity and effects at the macro level: material flows, waste, recycling, reuse, emissions, material footprints, spatial occupation, employment. More detailed indicators are available on food, buildings and housing, mobility and consumer goods.
Actual or intended use of the indicators	The framework and indicators are available online and will be further maintained and developed in the coming years. Targets on waste, recycling and material footprint connect to the framework.
Information gaps	Information on the transition process is largely missing.

European Union

In January 2018, the European Commission adopted *the first EU monitoring framework for the circular economy* developed as part of its 2015 EU Circular Economy Action Plan. It included a set of key indicators to track progress in the EU and in Member States (Mayer et al., 2018[53]). Most indicators were retrieved from existing EU monitoring frameworks, including the Resource Efficiency Scoreboard, the Raw Materials Scoreboard and the Waste Framework Directive (Moraga et al., 2019[54]). In May 2023, the European Commission published a revised monitoring framework for the circular economy (European Commission, 2023[16]). The monitoring framework is maintained by Eurostat and available online.

The 2018 framework included ten indicator themes and 24 indicators grouped into 4 thematic sections: (1) production and consumption, including self-sufficiency for raw materials, Green Public Procurement, Waste generation, Food waste; (2) waste management featuring a range of recycling indicators; (3) secondary raw materials, including End-of-life recycling input rates, Cyclical material use rate, imports, exports and trade of recyclable raw materials: and (4) competitiveness and innovation, including investments, employment, value added and patents.

The 2023 monitoring framework includes 11 indicators, some of which have sub-indicators, grouped into five thematic sections: (1) production and consumption; (2) waste management; (3) secondary raw materials; (4) competitiveness and innovation; and (5) global sustainability and resilience (Table B.9).

The framework provides a holistic view as it measures direct and indirect benefits of "becoming circular"; values the contribution of a CE in living well within the limits of the planet; and addresses energy and material supply risks. It has a strong focus on material circularity and on waste and recycling aspects. Other aspects of the CE transition, such as the link with climate and other environmental impacts are largely covered by other monitoring frameworks[1]. The intent was to keep the framework concise and to minimise additional burden on national administrations.

The following indicators have been added in the 2023 revision:

- *Material footprint*, measuring the overall use of materials and reflecting the amount of materials embedded in overall consumption, including imported goods;
- *Resource productivity*, measuring the amount of GDP from materials use and demonstrating the efficiency in using materials in the production of goods and services;
- *Consumption footprint*, comparing consumption to the planetary boundaries for 16 impact categories based on a life-cycle assessment and 5 main areas of consumption (food, mobility, housing, households goods and appliances);
- *GHG emissions from production activities*, measuring the GHG emissions produced by production sectors (i.e. excluding emissions from households) and reflecting the contribution of the CE to climate neutrality;
- *Material dependency*, measuring the share of imported materials in overall material use, describing how much the EU depends on imports of materials and reflects the contribution of the CE to security of supply of materials and energy and to the EU's open strategic autonomy.

All indicators meet the criteria of relevance, acceptance, credibility, ease of use and robustness. They were selected to capture the main elements of a CE. Communication around the monitoring framework also features an interactive material flow diagram for the European Union as a whole (Sankey diagram) and other visualisation tools with up-to-date data. In areas where policy targets exist, the indicators are used monitor progress towards achieving these targets.

Most indicators are based on official statistics sourced by Eurostat; a few use data from the research community. They are available at the level of the European Union, as well as for individual member states and updated annually. For some indicators, data are only available for the EU as a whole. The framework includes indicators for which data gathering is still in progress (e.g. Food Waste), where robust data and methodologies still need to be developed (e.g. Green Public Procurement or indicators in the competitiveness and innovation category). With respect to the latter, the documentation mentions the issue that economic statistics are based on industrial sectors, impairing a proper definition of the CE in terms of employment (NACE codes) or innovation (patent statistics). Patent statistics also have the limitation that they do not cover all innovation taking place, but only certain types. When appropriate, the Commission works with the relevant stakeholders to investigate the use of new data sources to improve measurement.

Table B.9. Indicators in the 2023 monitoring framework for the circular economy

No	Indicator	Relevance	Source
Production and consumption			
1a-b	**Material consumption** 1a. Material footprint (tonnes/capita) 1b.Resource productivity (EUR/kg)	Decreasing the consumption of materials indicates decoupling economic growth from resource use.	Eurostat
2	**Green public procurement**[1]	Public procurement accounts for a large share of consumption and can drive the circular economy.	European Commission
3a-f	**Waste generation** 3a. Total waste generation per capita (kg/capita) 3b. Total waste generation (excl. major mineral waste) per GDP (kg/EUR) 3c. Generation of municipal waste per capita 3d. Food waste (kg/capita) 3e. Generation of packaging waste per capita (kg/capita) 3f. Generation of plastic packaging waste per capita (kg/capita)	In a circular economy, waste generation is minimised.	Eurostat
Waste management			
4a-b	**Overall recycling rates** 4a. Recycling rate for municipal waste (%) 4b. Recycling rate for all waste excl. major mineral waste (%)	Increasing recycling is part of the transition to a circular economy.	Eurostat
5a-c	**Recycling rates for specific waste streams** 5a. Recycling rate for overall packaging waste (%) 5b. Recycling rate for plastic packaging waste (%) 5c. Recycling rate for electrical and electronic equipment waste that is separately collected (%)	Progress in recycling key waste streams is essential for sustainability and resilience.	Eurostat
Secondary raw materials			
6a-b	**Contribution of recycled materials to demand for raw materials** 6a. Circular material use rate (%) 6b. End-of-life recycling input rates (%)	In a circular economy, secondary raw materials are commonly used to make new products.	Eurostat, other EC services
7a-c	**Trade in recyclable raw materials** 7a. Imports from outside the EU (tonnes) 7b. Exports to outside the EU (tonnes) 7c. Intra-EU trade (tonnes)	Trade in recyclables reflects the importance of the internal market and global participation in the circular economy.	Eurostat
Competitiveness and innovation			
8a-c	**Private investments, jobs and gross value added related to circular economy sectors** 8a. Private investments (% GDP) 8b. Employment (% employment) 8c. Gross value added (% GDP)	The circular economy can contribute to the creation of jobs and growth.	Eurostat
9	**Green innovation** 9. Patents related to waste management and recycling (number and number per million inhabitants)	Innovative technologies related to the circular economy boost the EU's global competitiveness.	Joint Research Centre, PATSTAT
Global sustainability and resilience			
10a-b	**Global sustainability** 10a. Consumption footprint (index 2010='100' and times the planetary boundaries is transgressed) 10b. GHG emissions from production activities (kg per capita)	Consumption footprint indicates the extent to which production and consumption systems are within planetary boundaries. The circular economy contributes to climate neutrality.	Joint Research Centre, Eurostat
11a-b	**Resilience** 11a. Material import dependency (%) 11b. EU self-sufficiency for raw materials (%)	The circular economy contributes to the security of supply of raw materials and helps to address supply risks, in particular for critical raw materials.	Eurostat, other EC services

1. GPP indicator under development.
Source: (European Commission, 2023[16])

Table B.10. Summary of the EU indicator framework

Description	11 indicators and their sub-indicators grouped into 5 thematic sections (revised in 2023). Focus on material circularity and on waste and recycling aspects.
Indicator coverage	Production and consumption; waste management; secondary raw materials; competitiveness and innovation; and global sustainability and resilience.
Actual or intended use of the indicators	The indicators are available online. Regular (annual) updates of the indicators through Eurostat. Used to monitor the achievement of targets. Established targets currently focus on waste management.
Information gaps	Interactions with the environment, policy responses and social dimensions only limitedly covered. Some indicators require further work to be fully measurable.

Annex C. OECD approach to environmental indicators

This Annex presents key elements of the OECD approach to environmental indicators developed with the active support of OECD Member countries.

General approach

For more than 40 years, the OECD has prepared harmonised international data and sets of indicators on the environment, and assisted countries in improving their environmental information systems.

The main aims of this work have been:

- to measure environmental progress and performance.
- to monitor and promote policy integration, in particular, the integration of environmental considerations into policy sectors, such as transport, energy and agriculture, and into economic policies more broadly.
- to help monitor progress towards sustainable development and green growth, including by measuring the extent of decoupling of environmental pressure from economic growth.

The OECD approach to indicators is based on the view that:

- There is no unique set of indicators; whether a given set of indicators is appropriate depends on its use.
- Indicators are only one tool among others and generally should be used with other information to draw robust conclusions.
- OECD environmental indicators are relatively small sets of indicators (core sets) that have been identified for use at the international level, and that should be complemented by national indicators when examining issues at national level.

The work builds on agreement by OECD members:

- to use the pressure-state-response (PSR) model or its variants as a common reference framework.
- to identify indicators on the basis of their policy relevance, analytical soundness and measurability.
- to use the OECD approach and adapt it to their national circumstances.

The development of environmental indicators in OECD has been grounded in the practical experience of OECD countries. It has benefited from strong support from member countries and their representatives in the OECD Working Party on Environmental Information and its predecessor bodies. OECD work on indicators also benefits from close cooperation with other international organisations, notably the United Nations Statistics Division (UNSD) and United Nations regional offices (including UNECE), the United Nations Environment Programme (UNEP), the World Bank, the European Union (including Eurostat and the European Environment Agency), and international research institutes.

Definitions and selection criteria

Box C.1. Functions and definitions of environmental indicators

Functions

The OECD terminology points to **two major functions** of indicators:

- They reduce the number of measurements and parameters that normally would be required to give an *exact* presentation of a situation.
  ➔ As a consequence, the size of an indicator set and the level of detail contained in the set need to be limited. A set with a large number of indicators will tend to clutter the overview it is meant to provide.
- They simplify the communication process by which the results of measurement are provided to the user.
  ➔ Due to this simplification and adaptation to user needs, indicators may not always meet strict scientific demands to demonstrate causal chains. Indicators should therefore be regarded as an expression of "the best knowledge available".

Definitions

- **Indicator**: a parameter, or a value derived from parameters, which points to, provides information about, describes the state of a phenomenon/environment/area, with a significance extending beyond that directly associated with a parameter value.
- **Index**: a set of aggregated or weighted parameters or indicators.
- **Parameter**: a property that is measured or observed.

Source: OECD (1993), OECD Core Set of indicators for environmental performance reviews, Environment Monograph N.83, https://www.oecd.org/officialdocuments/publicdisplaydocumentpdf/?cote=OCDE/GD(93)179&docLanguage=En.

Box C.2. Criteria for selecting environmental indicators

As indicators are used for various purposes, it is necessary to define general criteria for selecting them and validating their choice. Three basic criteria are used in OECD work: policy relevance and utility for users, analytical soundness, measurability.[1]

POLICY RELEVANCE AND UTILITY FOR USERS	An environmental indicator should: • Provide a representative picture of environmental conditions, pressures on the environment or society's responses; • be simple, easy to interpret and able to show trends over time; • be responsive to changes in the environment and related human activities; • provide a basis for international comparisons; • be either national in scope or applicable to regional environmental issues of national significance; • have a threshold or reference value against which to compare it, so that users can assess the significance of the values associated with it.
ANALYTICAL SOUNDNESS	An environmental indicator should: • be theoretically well founded in technical and scientific terms; • be based on international standards and international consensus about its validity; • lend itself to being linked to economic models, forecasting and information systems.
MEASURABILITY	The data required to support the indicator should be: • readily available or made available at a reasonable cost/benefit ratio; • adequately documented and of known quality; • updated at regular intervals in accordance with reliable procedures.

1. These criteria describe the "ideal" indicator; not all of them will be met in practice.

Source: OECD (1993), OECD Core Set of indicators for environmental performance reviews, Environment Monograph N.83, https://www.oecd.org/officialdocuments/publicdisplaydocumentpdf/?cote=OCDE/GD(93)179&docLanguage=En.

Guidance for use

Box C.3. Guiding principles for using environmental indicators

The OECD has accumulated practical experience not only in developing, but also in using environmental and related indicators in its policy work. The indicators are used as a specific tool for evaluating environmental performance and contribute to monitor sustainable development and measure progress with green growth.

When using environmental indicators in analysis and evaluation, the OECD applies the following commonly agreed upon principles:

Only one tool

Indicators are not designed to provide a full picture of environmental issues, but rather to help reveal trends and draw attention to phenomena or changes that require further analyses and possible action.

Indicators are thus only one tool for evaluation; scientific and policy-oriented interpretation is required for them to acquire their full meaning. They need to be supplemented by other qualitative and scientific information, particularly in explaining driving forces behind indicator changes which form the basis for an assessment. One should also note that some topics do not lend themselves to evaluation by quantitative measures or indicators.

The appropriate context

Indicators' relevance varies by country and by context. They must be reported and interpreted in the appropriate context, taking into account countries' different ecological, geographical, social, economic, structural and institutional features.

Inter-country comparison and standardisation

Most OECD indicators focus on the national level and are designed to be used in an international context. This implies not only nationally aggregated indicators, but also an appropriate level of comparability among countries.

There is no single method of standardisation for the comparison of environmental indicators across countries. The outcome of the assessment depends on the chosen denominator (e.g. GDP, population, land area) as well as on national definitions and measurement methods. It is therefore appropriate for different denominators to be used in parallel to balance the message conveyed. In some cases absolute values may be the appropriate measure, for example when international commitments are linked to absolute values.

Reference values

Relating the indicators to reference values (benchmarks, thresholds, baselines, objectives, targets), helps users better understand the significance of the indicator values, and enables comparison between data that are otherwise not easy to compare.

However, the choice of the initial level of an environmental pressure and of the time period considered can affect the interpretation of the results, because countries do proceed according to different timetables.

Level of aggregation

Within a country a greater level of detail or breakdown may be needed, particularly when indicators are to support sub-national or sectoral decision making. This is important, for example, when dealing with river basin or ecosystem management, or when using indicators describing drivers which are relevant at the local level. It is also important when national indicators hide major regional differences.

The actual measurement of indicators at these levels is encouraged and lies within the responsibility of individual countries. At these levels, however, comparability problems may be further exacerbated.

Source: OECD (1993), OECD Core Set of indicators for environmental performance reviews, Environment Monograph N.83, https://www.oecd.org/officialdocuments/publicdisplaydocumentpdf/?cote=OCDE/GD(93)179&docLanguage=En

Box C.4. Quality criteria for aggregated environmental indices

Policy makers and the public at large need reliable and well-synthesised information about the environment without getting lost in detail. By combining the information contained in two or more indicators, aggregated indices make it possible to convey simple messages about complex environmental issues. Among their strengths is the potential to simplify the public communication process and to reach audiences that receive little environmental information at all. However, reducing the number of indicators by condensing information also runs the risk of misinterpretation because users are not always aware of the scope and limitations of the index methodology, and because the message conveyed may be distorted by data gaps.

At highly aggregated level, it is therefore appropriate for indicators to be used in conjunction with other indicators to gain a more balanced picture. It is also important that the aggregation process itself satisfies specific quality criteria.

Aggregation has been defined as "the process of adding variables or units with similar properties to come up with a single number that represents the approximate overall value of its individual components" (UNDESA, 2000). It requires a series of steps, that usually involve more or less subjective choices and judgements.

Aggregation steps

- Selection of variables that are representative of the topic, policy issue or phenomenon of interest
- Transformation into a common metric.
- Weighting of the constituent variables. This is the process of judging the relative importance of various components of an index. Weighting can be carried out in different ways.
- Valuation. This means comparing the indices with a pre-determined classification of what constitutes good or poor values. It is commonly used to present air quality indices to the public.

The aggregation process itself should thus satisfy specific quality criteria keeping in mind the intended use of the resulting index, and keeping in mind the quality criteria of the indicators: policy relevance, analytical soundness and measurability. Among the quality criteria are:

- The aggregation process must be completely transparent, i.e. every step in the process should be traceable. Users should be aware of all assumptions and choices.
- The variables to be aggregated should be independent, i.e. not show cause-effect relationship.
- The variables to be aggregated should be situated at the same step in the cause-effect chain. This rule excludes the aggregation of pressure and state indicators.

- All components of an index should be part of the problem and amenable to change in response to human intervention (e.g. although temperature is an important factor in ozone formation, it is not a valid component of an air quality index).
- All components of an index should show about the same order of magnitude.
- The conversion (transformation) of indicators prior to their aggregation with other indicators should follow certain explicit rules. Also, the rules for comparing the results should be defined before selecting an aggregation method (because the choice of aggregation method affects the message conveyed).
- Never combine objective (i.e. by way of accepted methods used by the natural and social sciences) and subjective weighting methods in the same step of aggregation.
- An index should be tolerant to inconsistencies arising from aggregation and valuation.
- As for other indicators and depending on their purpose, additional information and interpretation in context is required for aggregated indices to acquire their full meaning.

Source: OECD (2002), Aggregated Environmental Indices – Review of Aggregation Methodologies in Use.
See also OECD/European Union/EC-JRC (2008), *Handbook on Constructing Composite Indicators: Methodology and User Guide*, OECD Publishing, Paris, https://doi.org/10.1787/9789264043466-en.

Note

[1] The indicators in the revised framework are consistent with other EU monitoring tools, in particular the monitoring framework for the 8th environment action programme; the zero-pollution monitoring and outlook; the EU indicators for the sustainable development goals; and the resilience dashboard.

www.ingramcontent.com/pod-product-compliance
Lightning Source LLC
Chambersburg PA
CBHW061224240926
51846CB00006B/1343
* 9 7 8 9 2 6 4 3 2 4 8 1 7 *